D1797943

Romance & Dedication
in South America

DEAR ALL
The Memoirs of an Expatriate
(1934-1995)

a Novel & a Memoir

Romance & Dedication in South America

DEAR ALL
The Memoirs of an Expatriate
(1934-1995)

Angelo Capritta

Romance & Dedication in South America / DEAR ALL: The Memoirs of an Expatriate (1934-1995) – a Novel & a Memoir
by Angelo Capritta

© Copyright 2018
SAINT PAUL PRESS, DALLAS, TEXAS

First Printing, 2018.

All rights reserved. No part of this publication may be reproduced, stored in a retrieval system, or transmitted in any form or by any means, electronic, mechanical, photocopying, recording, or otherwise, without the prior permission of the copyright owner, except for brief quotations included in a review of the book.

ISBN: 9781791669386

Printed in the U.S.A.

To Charlotte and Lizzie

Acknowledgments

I would like to thank Margaret, my tutor at the East Warwickshire College in Rugby, for all her help at the beginning of writing, my wife June and my daughters Josephine and Margaret.

Romance & Dedication
in South America

Preface

"Romance and Dedication" is a short story based on the charitable work of several organisations around the world. The novel takes place in Central America and South America where the two protagonists, Chris and Pat, accidentally met three times in four years on different parts of the continent. It all began when Chris came to the rescue of Pat and the children who were returning to San Salvador's Mission when a severe storm severed the road they were travelling on.

One afternoon, on her way back from collecting the children from San Jose Elementary School, an unexpected torrential rainstorm made it impossible to continue the journey. She stopped at an old cabin where they took shelter. Minutes afterwards the road gave way and the jeep they were travelling in was washed away. An hour or so later Chris appeared looking for directions to the mission where Pat and the children were going. That seemed to be the answer to Pat's prayers. Chris, Pat and the children got safely to the mission where Chris, having delivered his goods, stayed overnight.

A few years later, Pat was on a transfer journey to Porto Alegre when a fault in the plane she was travelling in forced the pilot to land. They landed in Sao Paulo where by coincidence Chris was addressing an audience of about fifty people on world welfare. Although Chris had been delivering parcels the first time they had met, he was also one of the top people in the organisation. They met briefly in the refreshment room after the conference just to renew their acquaintance and have a chat.

A year after that Pat was taken to hospital suffering from malaria. Coincidently, Chris and a companion travelling up from Argentina had a car accident in the vicinity of Porto Alegre. Conveniently, they were taken to the same hospital where Pat was convalescing. This was the third unexpected encounter, but this time it was different. They had more time and more opportunity to talk. It seemed they were falling in love. After a few weeks they parted on the understanding that they would keep in touch.

Chris was later kidnapped, which he bravely accepted as part of his career. He was kidnapped by a group of freedom fighters apparently to retrieve a package which had travelled from the East to Porto Alegre by boat.

In due course Chris went to Porto Alegre, where Pat had been posted. They became engaged and eventually were married. Years later Pat met with a fatal road accident and Chris married Conchita, his best friend's wife who had lost her husband six months earlier.

Chapter One

Chris and Pat were married in 1975 after many years of contribution to the third world countries of Central America and South America. Pat served for many years with the Save The Children Fund and Chris with Medicine International.

They met for the first time in El Salvador in very dramatic circumstances. One afternoon, as was usual, Pat was taking the children from their school in San Jose to the mission in San Diago where they lived (a twenty mile trip which she had made daily for some time) when an unexpected torrential rainfall made it impossible to continue the journey. Pat and the children were travelling in an open jeep and besides the fact that the rain was coming down very heavily it was a chilly autumnal rain and, worse yet, they were wearing light summer clothing. They stopped at a derelict cabin, between the San Jose elementary school and the San Diago institution.

San Jose elementary school is two miles from the Honduras border as is the San Diago mission and the road Pat took runs alongside the border. They made it just in time. When they got inside the cabin and looked through what had once been a window, they could see the jeep sliding away in front of their eyes. In minutes the road gave away and the jeep disappeared with it down the embankment.

Now the rain was coming down as heavily as ever and there was not much daylight left. Pat had a real feeling of panic. The children were very good, most of them didn't know how near or how far they were from the mission.

They had no food or water, no light by which to see their desolate shelter; there were no tables or chairs, not a window to close or a door to shut. They were very afraid of the thunder and lightning and huddled together in a corner of the cabin.

"Now children," Pat said calmly to keep them in good spirits, "We will soon get some help. When they realise at the mission that we have not come back they will send someone to look for us."

Pat knew that no one would come for some time yet as she had taken a different road to the usual one and because of this she could only hope for a miracle. She had ventured onto a road which was a short cut to the mission even though she knew it was unwise. She wanted to make up for the time lost when she had had to stop to have a tyre repaired at a garage near the school. She had been late picking up the children and she didn't want to cause worry at the mission.

She continued to reassure the children and constantly prayed for help to come soon.

The cabin was inhabited by the most beautiful jungle birds they had ever seen, birds such as colourful parrots and parakeets, even a barn owl, and many others. The children loved it. The birds outside jumped from tree to tree waiting to go in. They kept flying as far as the window ledge and back to the trees wondering how long they had to wait before they could go and settle in their nests for the night.

Suddenly, as if in answer to Pat's prayers, a young man appeared at the window. Apparently he was aware somebody was inside, he must have heard the children chattering.

"Hello in there", he said as he saw the young woman and the children squeezed into a corner of the cabin. "My name is Chris, it seems to me that my road came to an end, perhaps you could help me." Then he looked again more closely to make sure he was asking the right question and then said, "Oh! It looks to me as if you could do with some help yourselves."

Pat stood silent, watching the man closely and listening to every word he said. She stood looking thoughtfully as she couldn't see what sort of man he was, whether he was young or old, or how genuine he might be. He had a long beard, was wearing a large hat and a soaking wet colonial suit. She realised at once that although he was speaking Spanish fluently, he wasn't a Salvadorian or a South American. He had an accent which she couldn't pin-point readily. She had to take a chance if she wanted to get the children back to the mission. She had never been in such circumstances but she knew that it was wise to be cautious.

"Yes," she said, coming forward and still feeling mistrustful. "We do need some help." She was being wary, she didn't want to be seen to be too dependent. "Who are you anyway?" the young woman asked without hesitation.

"My name is Chris," he repeated, "I am French and I work for Medicine International. I'm delivering some boxes to San Diago...."

"Thank God," interrupted Pat sighing, "for sending you to help us."

"...but I've run out of road, it appears as if the road ahead has vanished."

"Yes, we saw it washed away and with it our vehicle. We were travelling from Santa Anna to San Diago," Pat explained, "when the sky seemed to fall in on us. We had to stop and take shelter. Miraculously we found this cabin which minimised our chances of risk."

"Come in quickly, don't stand in the rain," Pat suddenly added when she saw how wet he was. "My worry now is the mission. When they realise that we have not arrived they won't know what to think."

"You can give them a ring if you like," Chris suggested, pulling a mobile phone from his pocket.

"No thanks, perhaps it is better if I don't."

"Is this man from the mission, miss?" asked one of the children.

"No! But he is going there," replied Pat.

"Do they know that we are lost, miss?" asked another.

"No, but we will be there before they realise."

"Where has the man come from, miss?" a little boy wondered.

Pat couldn't answer that, they hadn't got that far yet. After a moment of hesitation Chris looked at Pat and then bent down and talked to the children.

"I've come from Honduras, just across the border over there," Chris explained pointing towards Honduras, "and I'm as lost as you are, but now that I have found you we will go on together to the mission and in no time at all you will be sitting at the table eating a nice bowl of hot soup before you go to bed."

He took a bag of sweets from his jacket pocket and gave it to the children.

"Oh, they are wet!" the children cried in unison.

"Where is your vehicle?..." Pat hesitated not knowing how to address him.

"Chris, if it is alright with you," he promptly interrupted, "everyone calls me Chris. I prefer it. I'm driving a jeep-type vehicle, a little larger perhaps. It is just up the road."

"Yes, well, we need to continue down the road, and the problem is in the middle of it, as you know, and I don't think there is much chance of getting round it. I never should have taken this road you know, I never should have taken such a chance, putting the children and myself at such a great risk."

"Don't blame yourself, these things happen, it could have happened even on a good road. I'll go and take a look."

Chris went out to see how and if it would be possible to go around the crater.

"I hope his jeep is bigger than the one we had!" Pat exclaimed.

Pat had six children with her, and all but one of them, a girl, were under ten. She took them to school every day. The children were orphans and had been in the San Diago mission since it had been built six years earlier. The school in San Jose was an old elementary school taking children from all around Santa Anna between the ages of five and fourteen and many orphans from around the country.

"Here we are," said Chris, coming in after fifteen minutes quite excited and muddy up to his knees, speaking as if he had known them for years.

"That was quick, any luck?" Pat asked.

Chris told Pat he had had to go through some woods to get around the crater.

"It is not so bad really, I've seen much worse than that! Let's go before it gets any later."

"Good, and the rain has stopped," commented Pat.

"Yes, it was just a passing cloud," replied Chris.

"A very large passing cloud!" Pat said, laughing.

Now that the rain had stopped and it was brightening up a little they could see better where they were going. They got in the car comfortably although some of the children had to carry boxes on their knees. The vehicle was a large jeep, a Japanese fourwheel drive, and very comfortable.

Chris began to drive very carefully through the wooded area until they finally emerged to join the road some way past the landslide.

"Isn't this jeep a bit large just for you Chris?" Pat remarked as they were going along.

"Well, to drive through rough terrain as I do you need vehicles like this and believe me they don't last long either."

The road they had taken was very rough and quite unfrequented. It was not safe to drive along even in dry weather. It was used mainly for transporting farm produce by mule and oxen. Pat had known this but she had never thought it would be in quite such bad condition. Chris himself wondered how he had ended up there.

"It must have been the divine hand which guided me this way," Chris commented, "This road is not even on my map."

"I've been praying you know, and believe in divine providence," Pat replied.

Fortunately there were no other interruptions along the way. They arrived at the mission three hours later than expected, but not late enough to cause too much anxiety. It was not until they arrived that Pat's colleagues realised that something was wrong.

"What has happened, where is your car, Pat?" asked Maria, the matron of the mission, going to meet them.

"We've lost it," replied Pat without hesitation, "Sorry, there was nothing we could do. All I can say is, it could have been much worse."

"Perhaps when the weather improves and the ground dries the jeep may be recovered," added Chris.

"Weather? What weather? Am I missing something?" wondered Maria looking most surprised. She didn't know anything about the rain and the landslide, and of course she didn't know that Pat had taken a different route either.

"Oh dear, look at these children and the state they are in," Maria went on, turning her attention to the children, "and look at you, it must have been terrible for all of you. Go inside children, to Mrs. Rodrigues, she will give you clean dry clothes and something to eat. I'll help with the boxes."

Maria had been matron of the mission for some years. She was Mexican, and had been sent to San Diago when the mission opened. She was in charge and in total control of the mission in San Diago as well as San Jose elementary school. Now in her late fifties she knew the running of the mission inside out. She knew how to run it economically, within the strict budget of the establishment. Her experience in the service of the people, which spanned forty years, was admired by everyone who knew her.

There were nine staff to look after more than sixty people in the establishment and several hundred in the neighbourhood. Pat took care of the children. Juanita and Alvaro Rodrigues took care of the old and infirm. There were also two cooks, a doctor, a nurse and two nuns.

The establishment was founded and run by the Sisters of Mercy until Save the Children Fund took it over on the understanding that the mission should serve primarily the purpose it was built for - child care. The Fund extended it to accommodate the infirm and to a certain extent the homeless.

"Why couldn't Colin come?" Maria asked suddenly over dinner.

"It was a last minute decision to send me, replied Chris, "he was required to go elsewhere."

"Oh Maria," interrupted Pat, "I'm sorry I didn't introduce Chris to you, I was so anxious to get the children looked after that I wasn't thinking."

"Of course my dear," Maria replied understandingly, "I hope nothing serious has happened to Colin."

Chris assured her that Colin was all right and that he had been sent on another mission. She was very fond of Colin, he called in regularly delivering or sometimes just to say hello and have a drink. Maria has known the young man's family for a long time.

"How are things in Honduras, Chris? Are there enough personnel at the mission?" Maria asked.

"Things are not bad at all for the time being whilst requirements are being catered for, but there is a rumour that in the coming months we shall experience some shortage of certain unspecified items," Chris replied. "The personnel in Santa Rosa is adequate at the moment but in some rural areas it is very worrying, in fact we are promoting a scheme to recruit more staff. We recognise that over the whole continent we are working at seventy per cent capacity for lack of personnel. Europe as you know is the centre of recruitment but most of the recruits for some reason tend to go to Africa or the Far East," he continued.

"Surely there must be some explanation," said Maria.

"I wish I knew," Chris replied, "I wish I knew. The only thing we can think of is the ocean. It is like an epidemic, a hereditary disease transmitted from generation to generation, since early times when people only travelled by boat, and with the Continent of Africa being practically within walking distance they preferred the 'Dark Continent' and of course, the East and the Far East."

After chatting for a while longer they all retired for the night after such a tiring and eventful day. Chris left early the following morning but not before he had seen Pat and had a word with the staff.

Chapter Two

Time passed very slowly for Pat, she felt that she could do more, that she could help more people, but her hands were tied, she couldn't leave the children. Apart from the fact that the San Diago mission was short-staffed, there was no one who could take her place.

At the start of the new school year a new teacher joined San Jose school and she was given accommodation at the mission. The young lady, Juanita, was well known to Maria, newly graduated and this was her first post as a teacher. Maria knew beforehand that Juanita had been appointed to the school but she didn't want to tell Pat too soon because she knew that Pat was looking for an opportunity to leave the mission.

As soon as Pat knew what was happening she started working on how best to exploit the situation. She thought that since the new teacher was to be accommodated at the mission and commute every day to Santa Anna she might as well take the children to school with her. It worked out perfectly for Pat. She applied for and obtained a transfer. Obtaining a transfer in Pat's circumstances was not easy. After she had sent in her application to be moved the matter had to be very carefully considered.

Her reasons for wanting to leave the mission had to be approved by head office in conjunction with all those concerned and in particular the people within her present establishment who were trying desperately to convince her to give up the idea, at least for the time being. In the end the reasons Pat gave for leaving were so convincing that she won the argument, but it had taken up valuable time. She was sent to Guatemala for a time where she worked hard and passed on her skills but then asked if she could go to Nicaragua and then to Venezuela before considering her next move.

Looking after children was a large part of Pat's work, she was trained to understand disturbed children and knew how to deal with the physically and mentally disabled. She had a degree in Sociology and Human Behaviour. Her dedication was unique. After two years spent in various countries she found that the further south she went the more the people were in need. She moved on again, this time to Porto Alegre in the south of Brazil, and near the border with Paraguay.

She flew to Rio de Janeiro and from there boarded another flight to her destination. The plane, a light aircraft, developed a fault whilst flying over Sao Paulo so the pilot was forced to make an emergency landing at Sao Paulo airport. After they had landed - there were fifteen passengers in all - the plane was checked and they were told that it would take five hours to repair the fault.

By pure coincidence there was a conference going on in the airport press room on "Development and Ecological Concerns". Pat saw the notice board giving details of a talk which was currently in progress and enquired whether she could go in. This was arranged and she was given an identification pass and went in. To her astonishment it was Chris who was addressing the audience of about fifty people from all five continents on the environment throughout the world in general and in particular in developing and undeveloped countries, something he did whilst at the same time carrying on with his other duties.

Pat thought she recognised the voice as she entered the room but she wasn't sure where and when she had heard it. Of course this time Chris was clean shaven and was wearing a suit. When she sat down and then looked at the speaker she instantly saw that it was indeed Chris. She listened attentively as Chris was speaking.

"The men and women who came here before us," Chris pointed out, "were more concerned with poverty than with nature. As a consequence they failed to take any precautions to prevent the disaster we are facing today. I beg you, let's start today to try and salvage what there is left!"

Everybody was roused to give a round of applause. Then an official sitting at the side of the podium stood up.

"Thank you all for coming here today," he said appreciatively, "And very many thanks to Chris for his unprecedented speech."

It was then that Pat realised that Chris was a completely different person to the man who had helped her out in the storm. She was amazed and surprised, amazed at the role he was playing because she hadn't had the faintest idea about this side of his work and surprised because she hadn't expected to see Chris there. After the meeting everyone proceeded to an adjoining room for refreshments.

Pat was becoming more and more anxious to meet Chris again. She thought that it would be unforgiveable if Chris knew she was there and she didn't go and say hello, after all he would be only too pleased to see her.

She followed everyone, took a drink, and made her way to Chris. When she was about five metres from him he spotted her. At first he was not sure that it was Pat but when he looked again he was certain.

"Pat!" he called, "Is it really you?"

He excused himself from the group he was chatting with and went towards Pat.

"How are you my dear? I'm really glad to see you, what a lovely surprise! How long have you been here?" Chris asked while he was considering whether to shake hands or kiss her.

"Not very long, I came in towards the end of your speech."

She congratulated him on his speech and briefed him on why and how she came to be there whilst sipping on her glass of orange juice.

"This is an extraordinary surprise," Pat continued, "If someone had told me that I would meet you here today Chris, I would not have believed it, and yet here we are in another unexpected encounter!"

Chris looked at Pat happily and then said, "Really this must mean something, it calls for a celebration. I'm very glad to see you. Come, I would like you to meet some friends, one of whom has been in San Diago for some time and then we'll go and have some dinner."

"Thank you Chris, there is nothing I would like better than that but I'm running short of time, my plane will be leaving soon."

"Let us leave dinner then, but come and meet the man I was telling you about who has been in San Diago."

They went to meet Chris' friend Tom, who was more up to date with events at the mission than Pat was. He told her that Maria had left the mission to go to San Salvador where new and larger premises had been made available and where she would continue as a matron. Also the San Jose Elementary School had been transferred to the San Diago mission after they had taken over the adjoining buildings which had once housed the cinema.

Pat hadn't kept in contact with San Diago, primarily due to lack of time, she was directing all her energy on her work and was looking to the future rather than the past. She would love to have kept in touch but there just didn't seem to be the time.

As the time was passing quickly Pat thought she should go to check on her flight.

"Well, I hope we shall meet some other time and perhaps have an opportunity to have dinner together," said Chris, "I wish you a pleasant journey and the very best of luck with your new community in Porto Alegre."

"Perhaps if you are in the vicinity you will come and see us," Pat suggested.

"Goodbye Tom, it was so good to meet you. Please give my best wishes to everyone at the mission."

They shook hands and Pat went to find her flight.

Once Pat moved on from each of the many places in which she

worked she soon lost touch with people, it would have been nice of course to keep up a correspondence but it couldn't go on forever. She would have liked to keep some sort of ties with the people of San Salvador, Nicaragua and Venezuela, especially with the children, but it never seemed to happen. The only people she did manage to keep in contact with were her parents. Nevertheless, everyone she knew was always in her thoughts at one time or another, she never forgot those she left behind.

To give an idea of how Chris had started his career abroad, it came about that he joined the cadets at a very young age and he took his military career seriously. He had been educated in the forces, to the best of his ability.

By the time he was eighteen, he had changed his mind. He realised that there was something better to do in the world than to train for war, to learn how to face the enemy and how to defeat it with deadly arms. He resigned as soon as he finished his examinations, which coincided with the expiration of his contract. He received good grades and won a place in a military academy for high grade officers but he did not accept it, it was not part of his plan for the future.

Chris went to visit his parents to explain to them that a military career was not for him and he had other plans in mind. They backed his decision and hoped he would find what he was looking for.

Meanwhile he obtained a post, his first job in the 'civilised world' as he called it, as a journalist with "Dimanche Matin" in Lyons, France. This was a part-time job which allowed him time to enrol at the university of the same city where he completed his education. Soon he gained confidence and won the admiration of all who knew him.

After his graduation he went into journalism full time but this didn't last long. He resented having to write other people's stories, he detested having to write up what someone else from thousands of miles away reported.

He requested to be sent away, he wanted to see for himself how people were coping with life where war, terrorism, disorder and violence of all sorts were raging. He wanted to see for himself the refugee camps, especially where famine had taken root, and what could be done to help.

He wrote many articles for "Dimanche Matin". He reported marvellous stories, telling of things as they really were. He spent two years travelling all over the world. In the end he spent more time helping people than reporting about them. That was what motivated Chris most, to dedicate his life to helping others. Eventually he introduced himself into the world of beneficence which became his life's work.

A few minutes after Pat had returned from the conference she was told that her plane would be leaving shortly. She went to the departure lounge until it was time to board and shortly afterwards continued her journey.

The journey was lovely, Pat loved travelling and flying in particular, she enjoyed the entire journey especially the approach to Porto Alegre. The aerial views of the city and the surroundings were impressive and breath-taking, one of the rare views of South America she had seen.

She found the establishment to be just as she expected. She started work almost immediately. Soon she made a lot of friends, friends from all walks of life.

Pat was a warm, generous-hearted girl ready to deal with all manner of problems. She seemed to have been born for the job. She was always ready to share other people's problems, pains, miseries and misfortunes. She would do anything for others. She would share her food with anyone. She was passionate with the old, the handicapped and the infirm. She was sensitive with the children, especially the orphans. She knew how to speak to different kinds of people and how to defend what she thought was right. She was gentle with the poor, the weak and the less fortunate. She was hard with those who would not listen to the cause of justice, with people who had and would not give and with those who prospered whilst exploiting the poor and the defenceless. She was deeply disturbed by the growing number of helpless people and most especially by the abandonment of young children, a growing epidemic: the modern disease of the world today, Pat called it, without remedy or even the will to stop it.

Time at the institution was going fast for Pat, she maintained that time should be filled with deeds and things were not being done quickly enough to meet the needs of the day. Pat and her colleagues were looking after a very large area. Unlike the San Diago mission, the San Domingo mission housed the elementary school, a much larger orphanage and a group of decision-making benefactors concerned with the continent as a whole. Apart from being under-manned the mission was facing cuts on all levels.

In the summer of that year, although she had been immunised against common illnesses, Pat contracted malaria. She went down with it to a very alarming degree. She was taken to Pedro Cabral Hospital where she stayed until completely recovered.

After a week in hospital she was on her feet again though far from being fully recovered. When she was feeling stronger she offered her services where required. She had been granted the privilege of moving around the hospital and giving whatever help she could providing she looked after her own health first. She chose to assist in the most crowded area of the hospital where they were dealing with malnutrition. People were coming in or being brought in by the dozen, many of the children near starvation to the point of collapse. The shortage of qualified nurses made it impossible to give the necessary attention to all of them. There were many volunteers with little experience or none at all, some of them were ex-victims of malnutrition themselves. Pat's help was a great relief but had very little impact. Nevertheless her experience was much appreciated.

Late one afternoon Pat was resting on the balcony of her room overlooking the main entrance of the hospital, she was tired, and deep in thought and soon dozed off. Suddenly a loud, screaming siren from an ambulance pulling in woke her. She ran downstairs quickly ready to help and saw the paramedics rushing along the corridor carrying a stretcher. She looked and couldn't believe her eyes. It was Chris lying there.

"Dear God," she murmured, "another unexpected encounter."

She was very upset and angry. There was a lot going on in her mind.

"Is it possible for people to meet so often on such a large continent?" she was asking herself, "or is this pure coincidence?"

First Chris appears just when Pat loses her jeep, then Pat finds herself at Sao Paulo in the middle of a conference where Chris is giving a talk, and now Chris appears again in Porto Alegre, injured. So many chance encounters!

Was Mother Nature following them around and making it possible for them to meet unexpectedly with some happy ending in mind? Or was superstition having a laugh at their expense?

Pat was worried that Chris's appearance for a third time might interfere with her job. She had noted in Sao Paulo that Chris had taken an interest in her, as had she in him. After their last encounter Pat had thought about Chris a lot. She saw him as the ideal man for her, on the other hand she was not ready for commitment. She was twenty-nine at this time, in the middle of her career, and all she was interested in for the time being was helping the needy.

The following morning she went to see Chris, one leg was in plaster and he was resting comfortably, half asleep, but when the door opened and he saw who his visitor was he opened his eyes wide, as surprised as anyone could be. At first he thought he was hallucinating but then, since he knew that Pat was in Porto Alegre he was sure it was not the effect of the drugs he had taken.

"Well, hello again," he said, smiling and trying to sit up.

"Hello Chris and welcome to Pedro Cabral Hospital. How are you this morning?"

"I'm much better now, thank you. But what are you doing here Pat?"

Pat explained why she was there and Chris too explained how his accident had occurred. He had had a car accident a few miles outside the city, he suffered a broken leg and his companion had head injuries. Neither was seriously hurt but the vehicle they had been travelling in was a complete write-off.

"Well, I had hoped to meet you in happier circumstances, Pat, but I am very very pleased to see you."

"What were you doing in this part of the country?" Pat asked.

"We were coming up from Buenos Aires."

"I thought you had come a long way, judging by the dust you had on you," Pat said.

"Oh yes, and how do you come to know that?"

"I saw you yesterday when you were brought in."

"As I said we had been on the road for nine days, on and off. We had a few stopovers for rest, food and one or two visits to various establishments for business and also to see some old friends. We have been travelling for two weeks altogether. Yesterday morning when we left our last port of call and decided that when we reached Porto Alegre we would stop and freshen up and have change of clothes and indeed we did," Chris concluded jokingly.

There was a brief pause, giving them both time to take in the situation, it seemed as if for the moment they had run out of things to say. Pat looked overwhelmed, she couldn't hide her feelings for Chris and he could tell that she was preoccupied. She sat down. He used the pause in the conversation to reach for his pipe to have a smoke whilst thinking of something else to say.

"I don't think you can smoke in here Chris," Pat pointed out.

"It is all right Pat, just a puff."

"Now Chris, behave, have some respect," insisted his travelling companion who was listening in to their conversation from a bed nearby.

"Sorry Pat. Meet my minder," Chris said putting his pipe away.

"That is what he calls me when I remind him of his manners. My name is Roger, I'm very pleased to meet you. I've known Chris for many years, he is a good chap and a valuable companion."

"Hello Roger, "said Pat, "Happy to meet you, even in these circumstances."

"I thought you were asleep, Roger."

"He is a good sport you know," Chris remarked to Pat before going on to tell Roger all about Pat, although he had done so before. He told him about the circumstances in which they met, about the landslides, the vanishing of the jeep, the storm and so on.

"No doubt about it, I've heard that a few times Pat, about you, the children, the mission and so on and so forth."

"I hope he has said good things about us and me especially," Pat laughed.

"Chris wouldn't say anything bad about anybody, if he hasn't got anything good to say, he doesn't say anything at all," Roger replied reassuringly.

"Good man!" exclaimed Pat, getting up and preparing to go.

"I'd better go, my patients will be wondering where I am. I'll see you later."

"She's lovely, isn't she?" Chris remarked after Pat had left the room, looking for Roger's approval.

"Lovely!" Roger replied, "She is a very remarkable young woman, clever, sociable, pretty."

"And hard working," added Chris.

Chris was hospitalised for four or five weeks whilst Roger was discharged after only three days. For a man like Chris who was always on the move those four or five weeks in hospital would have been like Brazil being without sunshine for all that time. Nevertheless he had no other choice but to get used to it.

Pat visited Chris regularly for the next two weeks, before she had to leave. She was fit and well enough to resume her activities at the mission. She went to see Chris to tell him that she was now completely recovered and that she would be leaving. He was very pleased to hear of her recovery but on the other hand he was sad, because after two weeks of seeing her every day he knew he was going to miss her very much. He couldn't resist the temptation to express his feelings and came out with what he had on his mind.

"May I ask what your plans are, Pat?"

"First of all I'm going to catch up on the past six weeks, then I'll take it from there."

"What will you be doing, Chris?" Pat asked, as anxious as he, she could see that he had something on his mind.

"Well, I've planned out the next three weeks but where I shall be after that, who knows. I've been thinking quite a lot about plans for the future, in particular over the last few weeks. Do you think about the future much Pat?" Chris asked, in a quizzical way.

"Usually I don't, I'm too busy. Of course I think of the mission and how to get the best for all concerned. I think about my family and friends, things and people I grew up with, that is about all."

"Have you ever thought of starting a family Pat? Forgive me if the question is a bit personal but I think we have become close enough friends to be able to discuss personal matters. I hope I've not offended you in any way," Chris continued apologetically, "or caused you any embarrassment, you know, that is last thing I would want to do."

"No, you have neither offended me nor caused me any

embarrassment. I've been asked the same question before mostly by my parents and friends. To be honest, I haven't thought about it, I've never considered leaving my helpless flock, my career, leaving what I know best and what I believe in," Pat replied.

Although she was seriously committed to her job and her "flock" she liked Chris too and she liked the job he was in too, they were like minded.

"No, no, no, it needn't be like that," Chris interrupted when he became aware of how she saw the situation. "When you are in a job like this and you start a family," he continued, "you don't give up what you have been building up over the years, what you have achieved with your hard work. You don't leave your dear friends, you don't retire, but you increase the possibility of helping in the future, perhaps in the process there is a slowdown or a temporary lapse in the help you can provide in the meantime but in the end it is all to the good of others. For instance, if your parents or mine hadn't faced the fact that marriage is part of life's career you and I wouldn't be here today to help wherever possible."

"I thought you were a good lecturer!" Pat interrupted jokingly.

"Sorry, I didn't mean that to be a lecture. All I want to say is that I've been thinking about you seriously especially during these past few weeks and I would like you to know that there is a sort of love for you developing in me. Of course I know that this is not the time or the place for a proposal of this kind but it is very important to me that you know."

Pat did not reply, she was quite taken aback. She looked first at her hands, then she scratched her knee and her nose and then her knee again, before looking up at him nervously and kissing him on the cheek.

"Keep in touch!" she said.

"Shall I see you again before I go?"

"You will, goodbye."

She went towards the door looking somehow worried. She turned around, smiled, waved and shut the door behind her. She didn't give anything away. Chris now knew by her behaviour that she would be back and that made him happy.

Chris was thirty-seven, a courteous man dedicated to his career. He was strong and good looking with brown eyes, prematurely grey hair and the ability to fit into any walk of life. In fact he had friends of every different colour, religion and culture. He had a good background and tremendous ambitions, ambitions that had brought him to where he was. His parents had served many years on the continents of Africa and Asia working with charities of different denominations and Chris was very proud of them.

After four weeks the plaster on Chris' leg was taken off. Now he could move around and plan his return home. The day before he was due to leave Pat came to say goodbye.

"I found out about your departure and I came to wish you luck. How are you? You will be glad when you are out of here I guess and back at work."

"Thank you for coming, Pat. I'm not feeling too bad really," Chris murmured passing backwards and forwards in the small room with his walking stick. "I'm afraid I'm going to be on three legs for the next few weeks."

"I beg your pardon?" Pat said not having understood the joke.

"The walking stick, my additional leg!"

"Oh, I see," said Pat laughing. "I've brought you a book, it will keep you company on your journey. It is one of my favourites, I've read it a few times and I thought you might like it since you are going to have time on hands before you get back to your job."

"What is it?" asked Chris, "Has it anything to do with what I said the other day?"

"It is called 'Tarzan Adventures', it might or it might not have anything to do with what you said the other day."

"Oh! I like Tarzan, one of my favourites too," Chris said with a cheeky smile, "In my youth I read a lot of books, mostly adventure books like Tarzan, Spiderman, Black Panther and other photo stories with a bit of fantasy in them. I used to get them for my birthday and at Christmas, without fail."

"I stopped reading fables", Chris continued, "when I started University. Now you have made it all come back. Thank you for bringing it, Pat, it will make me feel young again, at least while I am reading it. You know it must be ages since I read a book. I mean books for adults, real books which you can get lost in. Unfortunately, due to more important things, responsibilities and commitments, I read very little these days."

The nurse came in to tell Chris that there was a call for him from Rio. He excused himself and went to take the call. After five minutes, he came back.

"It was my office, they have arranged for me to catch the early morning plane, at seven o'clock."

"Can I take you to the airport?

"Thank you Pat, you are very kind but it has all been taken care of, they have already booked a taxi to be here at half past five."

"Well then, I'll leave you to pack."

"My packing consists of my pipe and my toothbrush. Roger took all our belongings with him. So since I've not got any packing to do I thought perhaps we might have dinner together tonight, the dinner we cancelled in Sao Paulo."

"Oh... Chris, I'm really sorry having to say no again, we will have to leave it for another time yet again. I promised Conchita I would go visiting with her this evening, it was arranged some time ago and is work related. Conchita is one of my best friends and I am sure she wouldn't mind if I didn't go but I don't like to let her down. So I hope you don't mind either. Besides, if we leave it for next time I shall be able to look forward to it and I like looking forward to good things. I could have asked you to dinner at the mission but I didn't because of this other arrangement," Pat explained.

"I'm sure it will work out better next time. May I suggest that we leave it as an open invitation for when we meet again? There is another gathering like the one you saw in Sao Paulo, to discuss a different topic, would you be interested?"

"Yes, I would be very interested. Goodbye Chris... Oh! if you don't mind my asking, what happened to the vehicle you were travelling in? Is there anything I can do to help?" Pat asked with concern.

"Thank you Pat but I think we will leave it to the insurance company, they will deal with it. It was badly damaged and is not worth repairing. It could be months before they get the spare parts which are needed."

Chris was still holding the book Pat had given him and asked, "What is this particular Tarzan book about?"

"Well Tarzan, the mighty king of the jungle, was so busy trying to survive that he didn't show much interest in Jane. She stayed with him only because she thought they would make a good couple."

"Are you trying to tell me something?"

"Yes, you wanted to know what the book is about."

"What happens in the end?"

"Ah, the story continues in another book. Goodbye Chris," said Pat.

"Good bye. I love you," Chris answered warmly.

Chapter Three

Having closed another dramatic episode, Pat left the hospital somehow uncertain of her response to Chris's genuine interest in her. Nevertheless she had all the time she needed to think about it. She was not under any pressure whatsoever, she had months to think about it, time to talk about it, time to find out more about him and time to find out if he really was as interested in her as he seemed to be.

Back at the mission Pat's workload was at crisis point. She had to organise things for the plumbers who were starting work the following week, for the electrician and the builders who were already at work and in her spare time catch up with her paperwork. They were having solar panels installed at the mission, the first in Porto Alegre. It was a job which involved many tradesmen and a lot of traffic, dust and confusion.

And so time went by. Pat was becoming very anxious and tense. She had to find a solution which was acceptable to both herself and Chris, after all they were in the same profession. She talked with her colleagues about it but in the end it had to be her decision. She knew that Chris's admiration was something she couldn't ignore, something she couldn't disregard just because of her other commitments.

She knew that her commitment would allow her to fall in love and start a family without compromising her career yet she was nervous and therefore restless. She had been through all this before, she had fallen in love and it had had a painful ending, it had been a harmful experience. She had found it very distressing to have to choose between the man she thought she was in love with and the call of the needy. But back then she had been nineteen and the man she had been in love with had not been interested in her career so she had chosen to devote all her love to the people who needed her most.

Pat was an attractive and good looking girl with many good qualities and she had never been short of admirers but Chris was one admirer she couldn't ignore. She spent hours thinking about the situation. She knew that she liked Chris and that she had been in love with him since the day he had come to the hospital. In the end she came to the conclusion that she had no other choice but to accept the fact that he was the right man for her and that this was the right time for her to make such a commitment. Once she had finally made up her mind she was more restless than ever.

After some four months Pat received a letter from Chris.

"Dear Pat," he wrote, "forgive me for not writing sooner. The time passes so fast that I can't imagine where it has gone. First I had to convalesce for three or four weeks, then I had to try to catch up with the backlog of work which had piled up over the weeks. However, I haven't forgotten you for one minute. I must say that, despite the accident, Porto Alegre has brought me luck! Or at least I feel as though it has, knowing you means a lot to me, it has changed my routine, my way of thinking, even my diet believe it or not!

Last week we had the meeting I was telling you about. I've been appointed to manage the organisations all over the continent. That means from now on more work, more responsibility, and more travelling. How are things over there, Pat? Have there been any changes at all? Is there any improvement in the community? Are supplies coming in regularly? I'll give you a ring in a few days' time. All my love, Chris."

"It must be interesting, you didn't hear me coming," said Conchita, showing an interest in what Pat was reading.

"It's a letter from Chris," Pat replied. She looked a little disappointed, perhaps she had expected more positive compromises, more romance or perhaps a more firm date to which she could look forward, for which she could make some preparations. She could also satisfy Conchita's curiosity and tell the others that she was looking forward to something positive.

"How is he?" asked Conchita, "Does he say if he is planning to come this way? Or how his leg is? I would like to meet him, you know, after all that I've heard about him. He must be quite a guy."

"He said he is getting on well, he has been busy and he will call in the next few days."

"We are having guests for dinner tonight, Pat, did you know? They are presently looking around the premises. A man and a woman, envoys sent by the United Nations and responsible for Third World welfare," Conchita went on, "They are a very business-like, middle-aged people and very well dressed too, the clothes they wear are impeccable, Conchita commented.

"I'm not surprised," said Pat, "with the salary they get they can afford that and more."

"We are not complaining are we?"

"Oh no," Pat interrupted. "We are just being critical and very unfair to them."

"They flew in from Europe this morning. They will stay the night and tomorrow they will retrieve a large consignment which came by sea. It has been sitting at the Porto Alegre harbour since last month waiting for them to collect it. They will leave the cargo here where it will be distributed in due course under the supervision of high ranking officials."

Pat's eyes glittered at the words: "supervision of high ranking officials". She connected those words with Chris's promotion.

Porto Alegre was a very important central point of distribution for the whole continent. Being in the centre and within easy access of all areas by sea and by land it facilitated distribution, making it more economical and efficient. The consignment consisted mostly of medicine and clinical equipment to be distributed as far south as Buenos Aires, as far north as Sao Paulo and to the bordering countries in the south west. Pedro Cabral Hospital in Porto Alegre was getting a much needed share, partly due to Chris's recommendation given after he had seen for himself six months earlier when he had spent four weeks there after his road accident how much was needed and the great efforts of the staff to make do with the little they had.

Pat and Conchita had become very good friends, they frequently discussed their problems, their daily adventures and their plans. Most of the time they worked together as a team, they had many things in common including their background and their commitment.

Conchita, who was a year older than Pat and equally attractive and clever, loved her job and did it well. Unlike Pat, Conchita was looking forward to meeting somebody inclined to the service of the needy with whom to start a family. Indirectly she encouraged

Pat in making her decision and approved her interest in Chris.

"I should go and get ready for dinner now, those people like to do everything on the dot, we don't want to spoil their dinner, do we?" Conchita remarked.

Later on Pat and Conchita met in the dining room where, with the others, they were entertaining the guests. It turned out to be a very pleasant evening with vast exchanges of ideas, plenty of conversation and friendly advice, all in good humour despite the usual contradictions about some being better than others and so on and so forth.

The task of the two envoys, Manuel Cordoba and Mrs Helen Dune, was to take charge of the goods and hand them over to the mission until someone else arrived. This was the first time the consignments had been distributed in this way. Mr Cordoba explained:

"In the past this task has been confined to juniors and probably to volunteers, people willing to do the job the best way they could. For some unknown reason there were complaints about delays, missing items and papers being leaked to others. This brought in new regulations and, of course, more restrictions," he lamented.

He went on to say that no mission is one hundred per cent certain of carrying the job out undisturbed to the end, but that everyone would have to try to do their best.

Mr Menente, the head of the mission and the organiser of the evening, was there with his wife and his daughter, as were most of the staff.

"I agree with Mr Cordoba," he said, "on the idea of promoting more responsible people, especially when the merchandise is in transit between continents, on long or short journeys, but I would like to point out that if the voluntary help can't be trusted and therefore has to be kept under strict supervision the foundation will become more and more expensive to run, expenses will outrun our budget. Our finances are very critical as it is at the moment, I don't think the situation should deteriorate any further."

Mr Cordoba explained that what he had meant was, since voluntary work is based on part-time assistance the training the volunteers get is minimal, in fact, negligible compared with the training given to a full-time official.

"So what I would suggest," he went on, "is that we train people well before they are put on the job whether part-time or full-time, make them aware of what is involved and what it takes to do a good job. If this can't be achieved, then we have to accept the consequences."

Conchita expressed her concern about the crimes committed by such villains against the good will of others trying to bring a bit of light, a bit of hope to those people around the world who without it wouldn't have any chance of survival. She wondered what sort of people could do such a thing.

"People who fight for a cause they believe in," explained Mr Cordoba, "people who try to de-stabilise governments, people who profit from the misfortunes of others, people who are paid to stir up trouble and create confusion. These days," he continued, "there are extortionists and blackmailers all over the world. Take Ethiopia, for example, and many other parts of Africa for that matter, if aid was distributed under proper supervision it would make a lot of difference. I'm not saying that famine would be eradicated but people would live better and life would be easier for everybody concerned."

The following day, having retrieved the consignment, Manuel and Helen's task was complete.

A few days went by and still Pat hadn't heard from Chris. When she wasn't busy doing her practical work, she spent time catching up on her paper work whilst sitting near the telephone hoping at the same time that Chris would ring. She began to wonder just how reliable Chris was. She was becoming paranoid; she started questioning what Chris had said in Sao Paulo, in the hospital and then again on the telephone. Now that she had made up her mind about him she wanted something to happen, she was becoming impatient.

About a week later the switchboard put a call through to Pat. It was at last a call from Chris.

"Hello Pat, it's me, Chris, how are you?"

"I'm well, can you hear me Chris? I can hardly hear you, it is a very noisy line today. Anyway, carry on."

"On Monday morning I'll be arriving at Porto Alegre airport, the office will inform the mission in the next few days. It has something to do with the shipment you received a few days ago, I'll explain later. How is everything there? Here we are having a spell of seriously hot weather such as we have never experienced before."

Pat did not answer, perhaps she was not even listening. She thought, surely there must be something better for them to talk about than the weather?

"Hello Pat, are you still there?"

"Yes, I'm still here ... listening. Here it has been raining for the last two days."

"Well I'll see you next week, we have a lot to talk about.

"Like what?" Pat snapped, she was feeling quite frustrated and disappointed. She hadn't taken into account the importance of Chris's work and that he would be concentrating on his future assignments.

"We will talk about us, of course! I will see you on Monday."

"Well, I hope the weather has improved by then," said Pat rather crisply, "Goodbye."

Obviously Chris was in a really good mood. He was always adamant in his way of doing things, he always spoke his mind but he always thought before he spoke. Chris always adapted to the people he met no matter who they were, he was always courteous, kind and caring to people in all walks of life. He preferred to speak in an ordinary, everyday way which was acceptable to all.

Apart from this being his nature, the way he was, he believed that most of the people he dealt with preferred his down to earth approach.

Pat was different, she would adapt accordingly, depending on the circumstances she found herself in. Like Chris, she spoke four languages which gave her a great advantage in carrying out her work and she was given much credit for it.

Judging by the tone of his voice it was evident that Chris had made up his mind about Pat and what was more obvious still was that he had some sort of plan. After the telephone conversation Pat realised that Chris was still interested in her and she felt much more positive about their situation and their future.

Chapter Four

On the Monday that Chris was due to arrive Pat went to the airport, she wanted to surprise him by being there to welcome him. As she entered the lounge and looked up at the monitor she realised that the plane had landed ten minutes earlier so she walked straight to the arrivals hall where passengers were already coming out. Although she had been a few minutes late she knew she had been in time to see all the passengers go through arrivals.

Thirty minutes passed but she still hadn't seen Chris. She was clearly very worried now and bitterly disappointed and wondered what could have happened. Pat decided to go to the information desk of the airline concerned. The clerk on the desk told her, after looking up the passenger list, that Chris had disembarked and had come through arrivals.

Feeling even more disappointed and very concerned Pat got into the car and drove back to the mission, after first having another look around to see if there was any sign of Chris.

Meanwhile, at the mission, two men had arrived. One man introduced himself as Chris Murray and his accompanying friend as Pablo Martinez, a relief coordinator.

They produced identification papers and full documentation authorising them to supervise the distribution of the goods. Pedro Menente, the director of the mission, examined the papers and everything seemed in order although none of the documentation included any physical identification such as a photograph.

"Oh! How foolish of me, I didn't think of that!" exclaimed the man called Chris Murray, when he saw Mr Menente going through the papers again. He pulled his passport out of his inside jacket pocket and showed it to him.

"I must see Mr Martinez's passport as well," Mr Menente said politely.

When the formalities were over, the men asked to be taken to the warehouse to inspect the crates of supplies. They only checked two of the containers (which had been specially marked for easy recognition). Mr Menente was a bit wary of the two men but said nothing as he could see no foundation to be suspicious.

"Everything seems to be in order. We plan for the first delivery to leave the mission this afternoon if we can arrange the transport. We have been in touch with a local firm. They said transport could be arranged at short notice under the circumstances. The director of the firm, the Ultra Express Services Company, a short distance firm which only operates within a one hundred mile radius, said that they had worked for the mission for some time so there wouldn't be any problem in finding us when we are ready," said Mr Murray.

"Yes, we know them. They are reliable and efficient," confirmed Mr Menente, "But I'm afraid the paperwork won't be ready until tomorrow morning."

Mr Menente was an astute, self-confident man, with a lot of experience. He felt very uneasy and was fast becoming very suspicious of these men. Something just didn't add up.

The doorbell rang and Conchita went to answer the door. It was Pat back from the airport. She saw how worried Pat looked and without wasting any time Conchita informed Pat that Chris had arrived but she hadn't yet had time to see him. Mr Menente had taken him and his associate to the warehouse to check on the supplies and had everything in hand.

"I must go to see him straight away," Pat told Conchita, "I can't think how I missed him at the airport. It is strange and quite unlike him not to ask for me," she said, rather agitated. "At the airport," she continued nervously, "I saw virtually everyone off the plane except Chris yet the girl at the desk told me that Chris Murray had disembarked. Now you say that he is here but from the look on your face I am convinced that there must be something wrong."

"Perhaps we are over-reacting or perhaps there really is something funny going on; if there is we had better find out what it is," Conchita suggested,

A door at the far end of the corridor about twenty yards away opened and the three men came out of the storeroom.

"Here they come," whispered Conchita.

"Quick, in here," said Pat, pulling Conchita by the arm into a room near to where they were standing. She had seen at a glance that neither of the strangers was Chris.

"Neither of those men is Chris," she told Conchita, "not the Chris Murray I know, anyway."

"It's the one beside Mr Menente who is claiming to be Chris," Conchita pointed out.

Pat insisted that the Chris they were looking at was not the Chris she knew.

"Now, Conchita, there is something seriously wrong and we must do what we can before things get out of hand. I'll try to get Rio on the telephone," Pat said reaching for the telephone. She began to make the call but found that the phone was out of order.

Conchita was now very worried, and urged Pat to call the operator. Pat tried again but the line was dead. It could just have been one of those faults that sometimes happen on the line or it could have been sabotage. Tension was mounting, Pat and Conchita were growing desperate for they knew there was a lot at stake. While they were thinking and considering the alternatives, the telephone rang.

Pat answered, "Hello, this is Porto Alegre mission."

"Hello, this is Mr Pinhero from the D.S.A.C. (Development for South American Countries) in Rio de Janeiro, may I speak to Mr Menente, please?

Conchita went to look for Mr Menente, while Pat went to talk to the two men, telling them who she was and about her role at the mission. After speaking to them for a short time she knew unequivocally that they were impostors.

Mr Menente went to the telephone and asked who was speaking. The man at the other end identified himself as Mr Pinhero, the director of Rio's mission. He asked if the two gentlemen by the name of Chris Murray and Pablo Martinez had arrived and if everything was all right and whether the paperwork met their requirements. Mr Menente replied that everything was in order but that he would prefer the despatch to start the next morning due to the shortage of technical supervision.

Mr Pinhero politely pointed out that he preferred to start the despatch promptly since his men hadn't much time. Mr Menente assured him that he would do his best. After this conversation, Mr Menente felt a bit more relaxed. Hearing the voice of a man calling himself Mr Pinhero (which he knew to be the name of the director of the mission in Rio) had reassured him a little even though he had never met him or spoken to him on the telephone before.

However he still felt a vague sense of uncertainty. Having replaced the receiver he paused a while, staring at it with a distant look in his eyes. He stood there biting the arm of his spectacles pensively.

"Who was that on the phone Mr Menente?" Pat asked coming in, "Have you ever spoken to him before?"

"No, I haven't. Although he was very polite there was also something a bit strange about him. There is something not quite right about all this."

"I think that too, Mr Menente. Conchita and I agree that we must clarify the position."

In fact there really was something wrong. The man who claimed to be Chris Murray was in fact the secretary of Rio's mission and his companion was someone the gang had arranged for him to meet at the airport.

The day before the real Chris Murray had been due to depart for Porto Alegre he had unexpectedly been invited to give a speech at Brasilia University on the environment and the progress of green issues to date. It was a meeting which had been postponed from a few weeks before for lack of support. He had been contacted by a well-informed man who obviously knew the ins and outs of the organisation. Chris, who had been expecting to be asked to speak at short notice had seen no reason to be suspicious. He postponed his trip to Porto Alegre for fortyeight hours because the speech he was to deliver was very important.

The director of the mission in Rio had instructed the secretary to cancel the flight and to call Porto Alegre to explain the change of plan.

The men behind the plot had had it all worked out. It was evident that there was someone working from inside. They had tapped the telephone so that they could make the calls to Porto Alegre and to the airport.

Early the following morning the secretary of the mission took Chris to a small airport on the outskirts of the capital from where he would set off for the environmental conference. On his way back to the Rio mission after having seen Chris off, the secretary was stopped by two men and forced to drive to Rio International Airport where he was to board the plane to Porto

Alegre in Chris's place.

He was given all the necessary documentation, a new identity and was to be accompanied by one of the perpetrators.

Chris suspected nothing, for him it was business as usual. It was not until half an hour after take-off when the co-pilot came in and said that they had to make an emergency landing due to bad weather ahead that he began to feel that something was not quite right. He had checked with the meteorological station in Rio before he left and the weather forecast for the next forty-eight hours had been good.

There were nine passengers on the plane and three crew members. Eight of the passengers were to disembark at Nova Lima, one hundred and fifty miles north west of Rio where the executive aircraft was to pick up more passengers.

The plane landed at Barbacena, one hundred miles from Rio, on a deserted airstrip where, on landing, it suffered a minor crack to the tail flap. After ten minutes the co-pilot came back into the cabin apologising for any inconvenience.

"We will resume our journey as soon as we receive the all clear from the weather centre. In the meantime we will deal with a minor accident which occurred on landing."

The all clear that they were waiting to hear was to come from Porto Alegre when the operation was complete and not from the weather station at all.

"Are you sure it is the weather causing all this," Chris asked. "According to my report in Rio the next two days had an excellent forecast."

"We just follow orders, sir. We don't make these decisions, we just follow instructions and try to do our best. We would appreciate it if you would be kind enough to bear with us. Thank you. Now, would the passengers for Nova Lima please come with me. Do not forget your belongings."

"May I disembark too?" demanded Chris. "By all means, please do," replied the co-pilot.

Chris's impatience was mounting, for he knew that an hour or two's delay would make all the difference to the meeting he was to chair. It could jeopardise all the work he had done over the past months.

In actual fact the plane had been hijacked. The co-pilot, who was acting as a spokesman, was given instructions prior to every announcement while the pilot was kept gagged and under surveillance in the cockpit. The eight passengers bound for Nova Lima were put onto a minibus and driven to their destination.

The reason given to Chris for this transfer when he asked for an explanation was that, by sending them by road the plane could fly direct to Brasilia and therefore save time which would be to his advantage. He was not convinced. He asked about the passengers waiting to board the plane in Nova Lima for Brasilia. The man replied that they would catch the later plane. Chris did not think much of this explanation, he did not think it plausible. Anyway, he took a walk around the steaming, damp tarmac under the scorching bright sun.

Although Chris did not know it he was being watched closely all the time by members of the gang who had already been there when the plane touched down. He returned to the plane after a few minutes to find that it had been shunted into a disused hangar, the excuse being that the repair could then be carried out in the shade.

On approaching the plane he noticed that there was something odd going on, there were some strange movements inside the cockpit. When he got near enough he could hear that an argument was taking place. He moved towards the cockpit but was soon stopped and asked what he wanted. Thinking quickly, he asked if he could make a telephone call to Brasilia. He was told that Brasilia was beyond the range of their radio but he could try Rio.

After fifteen minutes the navigator pretended he had got through to Rio. Chris went up to the cockpit and called the mission where an answering machine clicked and said: "Sorry we are not here to take your call, if you leave your name and your telephone number we will call as soon as we can." The voice on the tape was Chris's own, he had recorded the message on the answering machine before he left, so at this point although he felt something was wrong he still had no concrete reason to be suspicious.

Of course he was not through to the mission, the hijackers had recorded the message at the same time as they had tapped the mission's telephone in order to play it back to Chris if he should become suspicious and try to contact his superiors.

Meanwhile, at Porto Alegre the delivery vehicle had arrived at the mission. Mr Menente and the impostor calling himself Chris Murray supervised while the supplies were being loaded. While this was in progress Pat, with Mr Menente's prior consent, contacted the police. She explained her suspicions. The police's first reaction was to check the telephone. It had undoubtedly been tapped so they warned Pat to carry on as normally as possible so as not to alert the thieves and to leave the rest to them.

When the van left the mission the bogus Chris Murray and Pablo Martinez followed it in a car that had been standing by. They headed for the Santa Maria Infirmary twenty miles to the west as they would have been expected to. An unmarked police car followed at a discreet distance.

When they reached the Santa Maria suburbs the car stopped quickly to drop off the bogus Chris Murray now that his part of the plan had been completed. Then they changed route and headed north west towards the Colombian border.

Minutes later the police arrived. Confident that they had netted the catch of the day they questioned the man, using that accusing tone adopted by government officials who feel confident that they have caught a transgressor.

"What is your name, sir? And what is your business here?"

"I am Pablo Martinez, the secretary of the Rio mission, a victim of this dirty trick. I've just been thrown out of a very uncomfortable large car. Presumably you know all about it," he answered, now in a really bad temper, straightening out his tie and picking up his Panama hat which had been blown off when he was forced out of the car.

"How do you explain all this?" continued the officer in charge pushing him against the car.

"Before you start pushing and kicking me around," insisted Mr Martinez, "I must warn you that you really have caught the wrong man and I really am who I say I am. You can verify my statement by calling our headquarters in Rio, and right now, before you get yourselves into deeper trouble."

This was Mr Martinez's second nightmare. Some eighteen months earlier he had been taken hostage by a group calling themselves Los Liberatores De Los Statos Pobre. Although it was a case of mistaken identity he had suffered terribly at the hands of the gunmen with a gun at his head all the time. He had been snatched from a telephone box when the group had shot their way out of the Banco Nacional De Los Suarez. They thought he was calling the police but really he was sheltering himself from the shooting. All this had come back to him while he had been in Porto Alegre.

Los Liberatores believed they had captured Ramon Cordero De La Cruz, a well-known detective responsible for the capture of several members of their group. In reality he had been on his way to the bank to pay in money belonging to the foundation. He was released when they discovered his true identity.

And now, Mr Martinez, an ordinary man who always tried to avoid trouble, was caught in the cross-fire once more. He was taken to the police station where, after contacting Rio, the police realised that they were holding the wrong man.

Having questioned him and taken his statement the police apologised, took him to the airport and put him on the first plane to Rio.

Meanwhile, a few miles away the van carrying the stolen goods crashed into a police barrier which had been set up to prevent their leaving the country. One man died instantly and the other was seriously hurt and died shortly after arriving at the hospital shattering all hopes of finding the key to the tragedy.

The crates which had not been checked by the men at the Porto Alegre mission were found to contain a large amount of money in American dollars (presumably money which had been laundered in the Far East where the shipment had started its journey) and fifty kilograms of new improved drug seeds destined for an unknown group in a certain country in the region.

The barrier had been set up, despite the previous orders, because it was the last chance to catch them before they crossed the River Camaqua. The two men who had travelled with Mr Martinez in the car behind the van, realising that they were running into a trap, abandoned the car and fled on foot. The police never found any traces of the men who had caused so much frustration to so many.

The drug seeds, which, after being examined by the police were found to be Nish, would have yielded one and a half tons at the next harvest at a value estimated to be around five million American dollars. Unlike other drugs, Nish could be grown in plant pots, like watercress, all year round. It is made into a drink like tea and used as a tranquilliser but it has devastating long term effects.

In due course the ringleader on the plane received a telephone call from his superior, informing him that their mission was accomplished, they were in possession of what they considered to be their merchandise so the plane could be released. He called Chris into the cockpit where the pilot, who had now been untied, and the co-pilot were being kept. The man took off his cap and, keeping calm, he said:

"Gentlemen, it is my duty to apologise for the inconvenience and distress which we have caused you but there are some things in this world which must take priority over all else, whatever the consequences, even things such as man-made poverty, man-made disasters, man-made suffering and other evils which man has brought upon himself. I'm sure Mr Murray can understand what I'm trying to say," he explained in a gentleman-like way. "I have just had word," continued the ringleader, that we have achieved our objective, you are free to go now. Thank you for your co-operation."

"Why have I been kept all this time without any explanation?" Chris asked, very angry by this time.

"We had to stop you from going to Porto Alegre and I couldn't give you an explanation because I didn't consider it appropriate, it would have upset our plans completely," the leader replied reluctantly. "Gentlemen," he continued, "I'm sure there are concerned people looking for you, so you had better be on your way."

"So, they stop me from going to Porto Alegre, presumably they send someone else in my place. Someone who looks like me? And for what purpose?" Chris was saying to himself. "What could there be in Porto Alegre which was so interesting to these men. Oh!" Suddenly it dawned on him!

"The cargo, the cargo in Porto Alegre, that is what you were after and you got it too!" he exclaimed looking the man straight in the eyes.

"Goodbye, gentlemen," said the man firmly, leaving the plane.

The plane took off and when it was airborne the pilot contacted Rio airport and told the tower what had happened and that they were on their way home.

Soon after the plane left the ringleader received another telephone call informing him that the whole thing had turned into a fiasco.

"Sorry, sir, the gentlemen are already on their way home," he answered, obsequiously.

On arrival at the airport in Rio de Janeiro the plane was met by reporters and the police. They already knew what had happened in Porto Alegre and were anxious to hear from Chris and the crew all details of what had occurred. The police took Chris and the crew to the police station to make sure they were all right and to take their statements. Shortly afterwards they were taken to their quarters.

Chapter Five

When calm was restored and things returned to normal Chris and his companion Roger went to Porto Alegre to supervise the distribution of much-needed supplies. They were met at the airport by Pat and Conchita. They were a little nervous and emotional which was not surprising at all after what had happened and all that they had been through. But for Chris it was a day like any other. He came out of arrivals as if nothing had happened, his head up, his pipe in his mouth, as jolly as ever and in good voice when he shouted from ten yards away:

"Hello Pat how are you?"

When they met he said, "So good to see you, Pat," he said, kissing her on the cheek, "Don't worry about my beard, it won't be there for long. Laziness really, isn't it Roger?"

"And it's marvellous to see you back Chris," said Pat, "What an ordeal you have been through."

"And it's lovely to see you again, Roger," she said.

Conchita welcomed them both and hoped they were well.

"How was the flight?" Pat enquired.

"Average, normal I would say. No kidnapping this time and no change of route!"

"Hi Pat, hello Conchita, how are you both? How is everything?" exclaimed Roger, interrupting Chris. "I've been looking after him this time, you know."

"Oh, Roger, my word you do look different. Mind you," said Pat, "when I last saw you you were in bed." They all laughed.

"Pardon!" exclaimed Conchita.

Pat felt a bit embarrassed as she explained the incident having realised what she had said.

"Of course you haven't met my good friend Conchita, said Pat, "Let me introduce you."

They shook hands, then Chris and Roger reached for the luggage which they had put down next to them and they left together.

"How did you cope in the hands of the kidnappers Chris?" Pat asked, as they were driving along the road to the mission.

"It was not so bad really, Pat, they were very polite, courteous and well organised. I didn't realise I had been kidnapped until the last minute when I was released. It was so well set up and so well prepared that I didn't have any cause to suspect anything, as I said, until the last minute. There were one or two things that made me wary but that was only natural, I believe," explained Chris.

"You must have been very angry when you learned what was really happening," added Conchita.

"Yes, I was angry and I felt a bit humiliated too, but then, I was thinking of myself, things could have been much worse. In any career, when you accept a promotion you take on so much more therefore you have accept the greater responsibility you take on. Of course, I never thought anything like this could happen to me, but I didn't rule it out altogether either."

"Tell me Pat, how are things at the mission," Chris asked, for the sake of changing the subject.

"Everything is running smoothly once again. We just got on with things once the ordeal was over," Pat replied reassuringly.

Driving along on the way to the mission Chris and Roger were remarkably observant. They remarked on new constructions, derelict buildings, unsafe roads, and many other eyesores. They wanted to stop at a building site, a project on which they were well informed, a complex of one hundred and fifty houses for the homeless and in particular large families. The project was financed by the International Fund, and should have been completed a year earlier but for various reasons there had been unavoidable delays.

When they reached the mission Chris and Roger were shown to their rooms. After a brief rest Chris and Roger washed, shaved and put on a change of clothes and then joined Pat and Conchita downstairs for lunch.

It was a well prepared and well received lunch and for a few moments all went quiet, life stood still, as they enjoyed the meal. Only the fan hanging from the ceiling with its soft squeak and the palm trees outside moved by the gentle wind disturbed the peace.

Having finishing lunch Conchita excused herself to attend to her duties.

"I'll just go for a walk," said Roger, perhaps sensing that Chris and Pat wanted some time to themselves.

Chris, taking advantage of the situation to be alone with Pat, seized the opportunity to broach the subject of marriage.

"Pat", he said, "Have you given any thought to what I proposed a while ago? Due to the short time I shall be here I have to ask you now."

"Yes I have, Chris, I have been giving it considerable thought," she replied earnestly.

"Then I'll ask you again, this time properly." Putting down his pipe he took her hands and said decisively:

"Pat, will you marry me?"

"Oh yes, yes, yes," was Pat's almost simultaneous reply, as if she had known what he was going to say. There was a pause, an emotional pause, they were both quite overwhelmed. Pat hadn't expected Chris to be so forthright this soon, and similarly Chris hadn't expected Pat to have her answer ready, so assuredly. They looked deeply into one another's' eyes, smiling, and then embraced and kissed.

Just at this moment Conchita came back, followed shortly after by Roger.

"Hello, hello!" said Roger looking extremely surprised when he saw what was happening, "What is all this then, eh?"

"Oh dear," added Conchita, "have we come in at an inopportune time?"

"No, of course not, come in, come in, sit down. Pat and I have an happy announcement to make. We are now officially engaged to be married," Chris joyfully revealed.

"Well, congratulations to you both! How long has this been going on? You haven't said anything about this Chris?" Roger said, looking hurt.

"It would have been wrong of me to tell you beforehand, I wanted to ask Pat first to be sure of her feelings."

"Many, many congratulations," said Conchita happily, "I am so happy for you both. This calls for a celebration! Just a moment, I have something special upstairs that will be just right."

Roger went to the sideboard guessing that some glasses might be needed and took out four champagne glasses and put them on the table.

"Four very delicate champagne glasses for this very special event," Roger said, most amused.

"This is for a very special occasion," Conchita exclaimed coming back again waving a bottle of champagne which she had kept for such an event. Roger opened the bottle and filled the glasses and gave one each to Pat and Conchita. Chris and Roger took their glasses and Roger spontaneously proposed a toast to the happiness of Chris and Pat.

Chris thanked Roger and Conchita for their support. "It is wonderful to have such good friends," he said. Then he continued:

"Tomorrow we shall begin the job which brought us here. It will mean two weeks intensive work so tonight let's go out for dinner to continue our celebration. Is that all right with you, Conchita, and you Roger?"

"That's a splendid idea, thank you," replied Roger, and Conchita was overjoyed and said she would love to join them.

At that moment Mr Menente came in to meet Chris and Roger. After a brief formal introduction Mr Menente was put in the picture and had a celebratory drink with them before they all went to start making plans for the following day's work.

The next two weeks were very busy. Apart from the work that had to be done, there were the wedding preparations to make. The wedding was to take place on completion of the distribution work. They could see no reason not to marry as soon possible.

It was becoming evident that Roger and Conchita were growing fond of each other even after such a short acquaintance and were courting too and making plans, thinking how they could best surprise Chris and Pat. They were planning carefully and in secret so as not to give anything away.

The distribution work took four weeks due to some unforeseen delays. However this was all to the good as it gave Chris and Pat some extra time to plan for the wedding.

When Chris and Pat had completed their arrangements Roger and Conchita unveiled their decision which stunned and delighted Chris and Pat and all who knew them.

So now the plans were to be extended to a double wedding. Having done all the planning Chris and Roger arranged to see the parish priest. They were finding their way to the church when the priest went to meet them.

"Hello Chris, how are you my dear man?"

Chris looked up, at first he couldn't recall who he was or where he had seen him before, but then:

"Padre, what an extraordinary surprise, it must be ten years now since we met last! How are you? And how long have you been here?" Chris asked, recalling the circumstances in which they had met previously.

"It is eight and a half years to be precise. Eight and a half years have gone by," Padre Alonzo continued, "and you still look as young as you did all that time ago. I was transferred here last year after the trouble they had here in which the parish priest died. I was sent here to replace him."

Chris and Padre Alonzo had met in Brasilia where they had been engaged in settling a dispute or rather a misunderstanding between the government and the Yanomani Indians over land belonging to the Indians and disputed by government officials.

"We took sides with the Yanomani," Chris told Roger.

"What happened in the end?" Roger enquired.

"Oh, the government gave in," Padre Alonzo replied.

"What a small world!" Roger remarked. "So you know one another, how extraordinary! Well it couldn't have worked out any better than having a priest who is also a friend to celebrate for us the sacrament of matrimony."

"Padre, my friend Roger and I, as you know, will be having a joint wedding. He is not a church-going person like myself, so as well as being excited he is also quite nervous as well," Chris explained.

"Not now!" Roger interrupted, "not now that I know our celebrant is a personal friend."

"Come," Padre Alonzo said showing the way to his office, "My dear friend, the Church is everyone's friend. It is a place which welcomes everyone when they decide to enter the temple of God."

Chris and Roger sat at a little table arranged in a corner of the small room while Padre Alonzo went to make coffee, talking to them at the same time.

"Staying away from the church does not necessarily mean that one has lost faith. People more often than not distance themselves from religious establishments for reasons of work, difficulties such as the absence of a church in the area, or lack of company. God knows everyone, and one day everyone will know God."

"Padre, I believe Pat and Conchita have told you about our arrangements," said Chris profiting by a gap while the priest was serving the coffee, "We came to find out if there is any documentation we need apart from the baptism certificates which I don't think we will get in time."

"I could help with that. If you tell me where you were baptised I'll do the rest," suggested Padre Alonzo.

"Thank you Padre, I would be so so grateful," said Chris.

"Thank you. I was very worried about this," Roger added.

"No need to worry, all is settled then," the priest concluded.

Chris and Roger got up, thanked Padre Alonzo again, and were leaving when he called after them, "And ask the girls to come to arrange for the flowers with the nuns. Goodbye."

Padre Alonzo De Meana was born and brought up in Spain. He had gone over to Latin America some forty years earlier soon after he was ordained. He was the son of the Count Alonzo De Meana de Salamanca who fought and was killed during the bad years of the mid-thirties defending the freedom of the country and the rights of the poor. Padre Alonzo had suffered considerably during the forty years of his mission, he had been morally abused, imprisoned, tortured and even expelled in some cases but like his father he never gave up his faith, his belief and the dream he had of seeing 'God's Children', as he called them, free and well cared for.

At last, with their assignment completed, Chris and Roger could now look forward to some time with Pat and Conchita before the wedding day.

Although only the girls were Catholic they had all agreed to be married in the Catholic church. Chris and Roger had been baptised but in adulthood had not attended services, although they had kept their faith and lead good lives.

The weddings took place in the church of Santa Maria de la Cruz Alta, in Porto Alegre on an April day, a typical South American autumnal day with dazzling sunshine warm enough to add glamour to the double wedding. All four sets of parents were present, and many of their friends.

The church, Santa Maria de la Cruz Alta, was built on a hilltop overlooking the pueblos down below and was itself a picture set in a beautiful spot. It had been built from charity money and the occasional gift from local authorities. It was completed in 1950 and had taken thirty years to build as funds regularly ran out. The name, which means Saint Mary of the High Cross, was chosen because of the distance from which the cross, which stands on the top of the church, can be seen, making it a visible point of reference for many miles.

After the honeymoon, which was spent in the nearby country of Uruguay, the four settled in the vicinity of the San Domingo mission, a temporary accommodation where life proceeded as usual, Chris and Roger travelling all over the country for most of the time, and Pat and Conchita working at the mission.

However, this didn't last very long. Within twelve months Pat and Conchita were both expecting their first child. That meant that the old plans had to be abandoned, their lifestyle had to be restructured and there would have to be an end to travelling altogether. The four of them decided that the time had come to stop running about and settle down, in particular Chris and Roger, at least for the time being.

Chris, an astute man ready to make the most of every opportunity which arose, had had an eye on a building for some time which had a lot of potential, for he knew the day would come sooner or later when changes would have to be made. He got in touch with his headquarters explaining the situation which the four of them were in. He illustrated the potential of the building he had in mind and the state it was in with plans he had drawn up himself and requested financial help from the foundation.

Meanwhile, without delay, he wrote to the local authorities informing them of the situation and enclosing copies of his drawings. Less than a week later the local authority had issued a no objection certificate which Chris received by post giving him the all clear to go ahead.

Chris's plans included the modernisation of the building - water, electricity, etc. etc. - the completion of an already started extension on the ground floor which had been abandoned five years earlier when decisions were taken to close the monastery, the cultivation of the adjoining grounds (five hectares in all) and the re-introduction of livestock to the premises.

The project was to be carried out mainly by voluntary work while Chris and Roger fulfilled their duty in the immediate vicinity due to their commitment to their families.

On completion of the project Chris would set up an office on the premises under Rio de Janeiro's supervision with the option of recruiting more staff to provide assistance on that part of the continent.

Initially the hostel would house, apart from the staff, twelve or perhaps fourteen homeless people who would help with the work on the little farm, the upkeep of the livestock and the odd jobs around the house. The farm and the livestock would provide the essential food for all the residents on the premises and hundreds more needy passers-by. Fresh water would be brought in from a nearby stream by way of a pipeline and pumping station installed with a purifier at the very top of the hill.

If Chris's estimates were right in ten years' time the operation would be in full swing. The four friends, Chris, Roger, Pat and Conchita, were thrilled by it all. They were really looking forward to it. The building was a seventeenth century monastery built by the Franciscan monks in addition to an old accommodation block previously built by the same order in 1532 when they came with the first settlers from Portugal, thirty-two years after Cabral discovered Brazil. It stood in a hilly area, sparsely populated in comparison with Porto Alegre, and had all the possibilities which Chris had in mind and more.

Santo Antonio Monastery was located near S.Antonio, about fifty miles from Porto Alegre. The old quarters, built in fifteenth century Mexican style, a derelict, typically off-white but characteristic construction of the time, of the type one can still see in some remote parts of Central and South America. They all loved that little building, they all took great interest in it. Chris in particular was fascinated by the way it was constructed. They went through some books and manuscripts they found in the newer building and traced the history of the place as far back as the eighteenth century when the newer edifice was erected. In the derelict cellar of the ancient monastery they also found a marble plate on which were the names of all the priors who had served in the area.

The first name on the marble was Jose Garcia, a very familiar name to Chris which he found very interesting. His mother's maiden name was Garcia and that was enough to interest Chris even more, for a moment he thought he had found the roots of his ancestors. With the help of Roger he traced the rest of the books which were at Novo Hamburgo where the monks had gone after they had left S. Antonio.

They didn't find out much except that Padre Jose Garcia was the first prior of S. Antonio and that he had come to South America with a group of eight monks, all but himself from Portugal, to settle in that area. He was Spanish and came from the Canary Islands. Chris's mother was Spanish, he had done some research some years ago and had got as far as the end of the fourteenth century, the discovery period when the Garcia family, a rather large family, and many other families, most of them religiously inclined, had dispersed around the world. To sum up, the chances were that Chris had found out that one of his ancestors had founded the Santo Antonio Monastery.

Chris maintained that the potential of the building was tremendous, that there were a lot of avenues which could be explored including a school for under-privileged children.

Once the establishment was in operation it could be used as a holiday place with facilities for convalescents and the profits could easily pay for the upkeep of the place or it could be diverted to other good uses.

Chris's ideas were great, he always planned for the four of them, after all they were in the same circumstances, they all liked one another, they all liked the job they were doing, the people they were dealing with and the climate which was the best in that part of the country. Their future depended vastly on Chris's project.

For the four of them life proceeded as expected, carrying out their work and starting families. They were never far apart, their friendship never lapsed. Chris and Pat had three children of their own, one girl and two boys. Later they adopted two more girls. Conchita and Roger had one boy of their own and like Chris and Pat they adopted two girls.

Shortly after they were married, they took up the challenge of restoring a large derelict house which previously had been run by the Benedictine monks. It had been closed down because the number of monks living there had fallen sharply and therefore it was too expensive to run. The order had intended to sell it in due course and divert the money to other establishments but because Chris, Pat, Roger, and Conchita had taken on the challenge for the benefit of the people of the pueblo, the building remained the property of the Order. It was a big project, the work to be done was long and painstaking, the more they did, the more needed to be done. Nevertheless, they never gave up for they had known all along what they had taken on. There were plenty of volunteers willing to lend a hand and do whatever there was to be done.

Pablo, the gardener who was there doing what he could, was looking forward to the completion of the work, as were all the residents of the pueblo.

Pablo was an old man who had lived there practically all his life except during the two great wars. He had no family and no relatives but he had a lot of friends. His parents died when he was still a young boy. The monks had taken care of him in the monastery where he had spent many years. When the monks left he stayed behind to look after the building until they decided what to do with it.

For him, when Chris, Pat, Roger and Conchita took over, those days, weeks, months and years of renovating were like the beginning of a new life.

Whenever he could, whenever he had a chance to chat, he talked about nothing else but the two world wars he had fought in, the places he had been to and the people he had known around the world. He told them tales of people they had never heard of before and of places they didn't know existed. Poor Pablo, in the end only Chris had enough patience to listen to him, he had bored all the others with his stories day in and day out.

After ten years of happy marriage and the years spent working together on the buildings, tragedy was about to strike. Roger contracted a disease, a type of yellow fever. He bravely fought the disease but to no avail. He could not be saved and died after a few months. Conchita was devastated but she knew that for the children's sake she would have to carry on and face the future without Roger.

Chris and Pat and everyone at the old monastery were in a state of shock but they were a solid group of people and supported one another and looked to the future. They all carried on with the continuous work but always with Roger in their thoughts.

Another tragedy was soon to occur. Six months later Pat met with a fatal car accident.

Everyone was in a state of shock and disbelief and initially Chris thought his world had come to an end.

So many thoughts crowded into his head: how would he cope with the children, supporting them in their own grief, and how would he be able to concentrate on plans for the future?

When Roger died Chris felt it very deeply. It was like losing a brother. He had been Chris's right hand in all respects, a much valued friend and a good support wherever he decided to go and whatever he decided to do. His death dealt a terrible blow to Chris. Apart from the commitments they had entered into together which Chris now had to carry out no matter what, he had the task of looking after Roger's children and making sure that they got the best he could give. Roger, an energetic, enthusiastic and active man had loved his job and had done it well. Like the others he was always the first to jump to his feet whenever there was something to do or somewhere to go.

He was a coloured man of North African origin who had been adopted by a couple of mixed race when he was seven years of age. He had been moving from one refugee camp to another for more than four years when he was first taken in by foster parents who later adopted him. He was born in Algeria in 1942. His parents were killed soon after the war when unrest between the Arabs and the occupying forces (then the colonial French troops) increased to an unprecedented proportion.

Roger's adoptive parents where part of a negotiating party trying to find a solution to the conflict between the two rival countries. They decided to foster Roger after touring several camps where thousands of children, supervised by various charities, were desperately yearning for help. Although Roger was very young he never forgot what it was like in those days. He never forgot the misery. And he also never forgot the help that was received from missions and what it meant to all of them. Without such help surely many of them would have met starvation. That was one of the main reasons why Roger had joined the foundation soon after he had finished his education.

Conchita's aim was different. She had wanted to be an actress, a drama player. At college she had done well, she studied arts which fulfilled her ambitions. Soon after graduation she starred in the film "The Hidden Children", her very first film and it was to be her last. The film was shot on location on the Central American island of Coiba. Conchita played the protagonist, a nun taking in forgotten children in the most remote areas of the island.

When the film was completed she realised that there was more real-life drama than she could ever act out. She maintained that all life was drama. There were many more people in need of help than the script had suggested. She appreciated the message of the script, its contents and the efforts the producer had put into it. She learned from it what she never could have comprehended from the stage.

She requested permission from Mr Consalo, the producer, to stay on the island for a long holiday to give her time to think and decide what her future was going to be. She had two questions in mind, crucial questions. Should she act and pretend to do some good through the script? Or should she become a real-life benefactor, write her own "script" in her own words?

After six months she returned to her producer only to say that she had made up her mind to leave the film industry as soon as she was permitted to do so. She applied to an organisation and before the end of the year she had been posted to the island she had chosen, where with the help of senior colleagues she built up her confidence and gained experience before she moved to Porto Alegre.

Chris and Roger had spent twenty years of their lives assisting one another, twenty years of travelling together and twenty years of hard work sometimes in desperate circumstances desperately helping others. Together they had met all types of people: good people, benefactors, and the poor and hungry who had nothing and nowhere to go; but also the bad and greedy, the vicious, the malicious, people who had and wanted more.

When Pat died Chris reached breaking point. He fell into a silent coma; for a while he didn't want to see anybody (except Conchita and the children), he didn't want to know about work and the correspondence which went with it which took up a large part of every morning. He disconnected the telephone in his office and gave orders to the staff that he was not to be disturbed whatever the circumstances. Conchita looked after the emergencies, he only wanted to be left alone. And yet, he knew that life must go on, that the clock couldn't be turned back and that we all are vulnerable.

Being a good Christian helped him a lot to understand the fact of life that men must accept whatever is sent from above. He was angry but only with circumstances; he hated nobody. Conchita was around most of the time looking after the children - she only lived downstairs - so getting the food ready and looking after the children was not a problem. Conchita did whatever she could to persuade Chris to put the past behind him and emerge again into the public life for the sake of the children and his mission in life.

"I guess I'm not the only one, am I Conchita? I mean I'm not the only one who lost his wife? After all you have lost Roger and you have been courageous and carry on, although I understand that you will never get over the loss. No, I am really not the only one in such circumstances. What do the others do that I cannot do?

But then not everybody dies the same way Pat did, without any warning. What do you think Conchita?" wondered Chris.

"I think I can see the old Chris re-emerging gradually. It is a great relief to me, what I've been waiting for, it is the same relief I felt after Roger's death when you talked me out of my low ebb," Conchita answered.

"Roger was my dear friend as you all are, he wouldn't have wanted to see you looking like you did, he wanted everybody to be happy no matter what the circumstances, he knew that life is too short to be sad."

"Exactly," Conchita interrupted, "Why be sad when we know that life is a gift to us from God, to be taken back whenever he decides it is time. Nevertheless we must remember those who go before us and pray for their eternal rest. We must also remember to look after our own life and not neglect it, for we are responsible for it.

"What makes me angry most of all is that, for all the good we have done and continue to do, we have been rewarded with unfairness. Who is going to be next I wonder?" Chris sighed.

"Dinner is on the table!" shouted Conchita loud enough for the children to hear in the playroom.

The children responded at once, leaving their playtime. They all sat at the table, all ten of them. Conchita thanked God for the food that they were about to receive and only when they all answered "Amen" could they start eating.

"Father," said the eldest of Chris's boys while they were eating, "Mrs Garcia said that mother is in heaven."

"Yes, my boy," said Chris, somewhat taken by surprise, "She is up there looking down on us.

"Does everybody go to heaven when they die, father?" the other boy wondered.

"No, I believe not," replied Chris, "but most do, people with good qualities and who have lived a good life and your mother had many good qualities," Chris answered. "Now let's eat and when we have finished we will all go for a ride and have a walk up on the hills," Chris suggested to change the subject.

It was a week since they had last been out, not since Pat's funeral, it was about time they went for a breath of fresh air. It was especially important for Chris to emerge into the daylight and give a boost to the little community he had built up whose confidence and morale was at its lowest, a community which had so much confidence in him and he in it.

The community in Santo Antonio was now showing signs of the hard work they had all put into it, the outcome of the good and strong will they all had towards it. Chris's plans had for the most part come to fruition: the supply of manpower, the finances from different sources, the collaboration of the local authorities and the benefits it was now offering. All this gave everyone cause to be proud.

There were some setbacks with the water supply. Unforeseeably Chris had to face the fact that the stream from which they were drawing their water might at some time in the future dry up. Just as his project was coming to completion, another project was taking shape. Twenty miles upstream an irrigation programme was underway and was taking up half of the stream's flow, causing a shortage at Santo Antonio. This would create a problem especially during the summer months and Chris was under pressure to find an alternative. He had considered two options: one, to build another pipeline some miles away, the other, to dig a well.

A well would require the assistance of highly skilled and technical expertise and sophisticated machinery whilst the pipeline, although much longer than the previous one, would be cheaper, simpler and quicker, but the danger of the water supply being cut again in the future would remain. It was decided that whilst plans were being drawn up and they were considering which of the two plans to adopt and who would provide the money (because this time they were talking about a large amount of money), they decided that they would have the water supplied by tanker when shortages occurred.

By the eighth anniversary of the start of work on Chris's far-sighted plans, the complex was functioning as expected, except for some small things like an extra bathroom, the odd cupboard, tidying up the garden, the drive or planting a few trees here and there. They had the livestock they wanted, including cows for the milk and cheese they needed and chicken for the meat and eggs required. The land provided grain for flour, vegetables and fruit. There were enough personnel to cultivate quite a large area. They didn't want any more disasters.

Conchita and Chris continued to support one another in all things but especially with the care of their children. They gradually found that looking after the children was getting harder every day, particularly for Chris who had taken so much on.

After several months they realised how much they had in common: the loss of their respective spouses, the children, their way of life and the disastrous period they have been through. The respect they had for one another which had grown over years of togetherness and friendship was enormous and therefore they were inseparable.

It seemed as if at last providence was shining on them and their lives had fallen into place once again.

After a great deal of thought they made up their minds and decided to marry.

After all, Pat and Roger would have wanted them to be happy!

DEAR ALL
The Memoirs of an Expatriate
1934-1995

For my family and friends and my home town of Serradifalco in Sicily.

Preface

In 1988, I came to the conclusion that my English was not what it should be after so many years in English speaking countries. I decided that an English course would improve my writing (and my spelling which at times I couldn't read myself).

In the autumn of that year I enrolled on an evening course at the East Warwickshire College in Rugby. It was a weekly evening class, "The English Workshop". It was the sort of course I wanted. The tutor was a good one, a lady with a good understanding and many years of experience. Margaret (the tutor) was confident with her work. Gradually she helped me and others to put right what was wrong with our spelling and grammar.

There were only nine of us in the class so the tutor was available to look at our work whenever needed. In the workshop we had word processors on which most of the work was done.

The idea of this book grew from excitement and anxiety. Excitement because now I was somehow writing in English. Anxiety because I could write down what I had wanted to for such a long time. Anxiety and concern which I felt about my family, my friends and my town which I left behind so many years ago.

So I had the idea of writing my memoirs, memoirs that span forty-five years of my life at home and abroad; memoirs which I hoped very much to become a book, a book that I would like to reach all the people taking part in it and more.

This true story has kept me writing for more than two years. The thought of my family, my town of Serradifalco, "my town" and my friends, to whom I dedicate this book, kept me writing and thinking for such a long time, recalling dates, places, and names.

I also dedicate this book to everyone who directly and indirectly participated in this summary of my life and theirs. It gave me great pleasure, the outcome I produced for others and for myself.

Many books have been written through the years, by exiles, emigrants or runabouts, but to my knowledge, this story is unique, unique because it is real, nothing added or omitted.

There are two parts to the story, running parallel from the beginning to the end.

One is the story of my family, my friends, my town and me; the other a biography of the work in the town and what it took to exhaust the vast underground deposits and the centuries of history of the town in question.

Some of the people and place names in local language give an authentic feeling.

The thought of how the 'serradifalchesi' - the people from Serradifalco - could have prevented the closure of the only industry in the area, came to an end when I realised that I was worrying too much, while the 'paesani', the fellow countrymen and women were enjoying life and taking it as it came. Perhaps it was my little contribution to the works that kept me anxious all this time in the hope that things would change the outcome.

This true story, in my opinion, is the average experience of a man or a woman who leaves his or her home town, with the exception that this, to my knowledge, is the first time it has been written in detail and in plain English for everyone who wishes to read it.

Places and names of persons are accurate to the nearest detail; locations and figures to the best of my knowledge.

Now... I would like to thank June, my wife, who helped with spelling, Jo and Margaret my daughters with editing and encouragement.

Dear All

It was not until 1943 that I began to understand about the war and what the war was about. News was scarce. There was one newspaper reader per one hundred people, (called a "Fanatic"). He used to pass the news (what he read) around through clubs, friends and in the public squares. It spread like wildfire. It went from one end of the town to the other.

By the time it got there it had a bit missing or a bit more than it had originally. At the time I was ten years old and I hardly knew what was going on. Everybody was looking forward to the end of the war; the creation of jobs and the end of misery. This was the preaching of the pro-allies. Great freedom of speech, freedom of choice and freedom to emigrate.

The Fascists, on the other hand, were insisting that only if we won the war could we have all this. This was the argument going on all the time, in the streets and among some families, sometimes with sad endings. Although I was not old enough to understand what was going on I was very apprehensive. I understood that the Americans were advancing and that the American aeroplane had two tails (this enabled me to identify aeroplanes flying over), and the Axis were not doing well.

One day in the late spring the teacher took the class for a day out in the country, the sky was blue, the sun was shining and the air warm. It was perfect for a lie down. All of a sudden from the horizon appeared this big noisy aeroplane.

"Americans, they are Americans!" I shouted.

The teacher was looking at me as if to say, "And what do you know?"

"They've got two tails have they not," I explained.

The teacher himself was a Fascist (at the time teachers were Fascists or pretended to be in order to hold onto the job). In his metamorphosis into a good man, when he knew that the Fascist regime was rapidly declining, I got away with just a look, otherwise it would have been a lecture.

Before long the Allies invaded Sicily, landing at Licata. The people in town heard the news almost immediately. Some were happy and some were sad but everyone was afraid of what would happen next, in fact the same day some cannon shells start raining around the town.

Everybody left the town, they took what they could and fled on foot, by car, on horseback, on bikes and by whatever transport was available taking what they could with them.

Everybody evacuated to the countryside where they stayed for eight days with very little water and food, all holed in caves, in barns, and wherever they could hide to minimise the risk of being seen in the open air. Really there was no risk as far as we were away from the built-up area. I remember my paternal grandfather sitting under an olive tree all day long, determined to stay out from five am to ten pm. He was very happy with his pipe, smoking continually. From time to time I kept him company while he was telling me stories from around the world. He was eighty-two at the time and he knew a few very entertaining stories.

My other grandfather on my mother's side, Mirisola, was out and about on the farm gathering produce and looking after the livestock, providing food and water, since they could not graze in the open to avoid being seen by the enemy for the full 9 days we were in the countryside hiding.

Licata, in the south east of Sicily, is twenty-five miles from Serradifalco. It took the Americans eight days to remove eight Germans and two cannon posted on the top of a hill, well camouflaged and determined to hold the enemy back.

After a week of shooting back and forward the Germans realised that it was time to call it a day, left what they had and fled northward. The Americans entered the town, a ghost town, otherwise undamaged except a few windows shattered by cannon shells that exploded nearby.

Before long Sicily was liberated, but it was eighteen months later when the whole of Italy was set free. Before that came the announcement of Mussolini's death, which brought relief for most of the people who had suffered under him.

With the end of the war there was freedom of speech, freedom of choice and freedom to emigrate. For the next decade there was not much to choose from and nothing to speak of, but the emigration dream became a reality.

The economy in the following years was very stagnant. There was no quick solution; hope was the only relief. Misery had taken possession; it was there to stay. It had hurt the poor very badly.
For Serradifalco and towns like it, it was not as bad as some of the more agricultural places. Serradifalco had been a mining town for centuries with large deposits of sulphur of many grades.

When the war ended, the struggle for power began. There were a dozen political parties which had to fight hard to gain the public's support, aligning themselves to take on the government. There was unrest all over the country.

Communists and Socialists rallied behind the red flag under the emblem of the hammer and sickle, chanting; "Down with the capitalists and long live Baffone". Baffone was Stalin; the reds were hoping to adopt his doctrine and carry out his Manifesto. Of course most of the followers were ignorant, they thought that the Communists would provide jobs. That was in the morning.

In the afternoon, the Christian Democrats, behind the white flag, chanted, "Long live the freedom of Italy."

The industrial workers were asking for a bigger share of the profits. The peasants were demanding a share of land, going from farm to farm carrying banners and showing determination.

They were claiming that the land belonged to the peasants and that it should be divided between them. That never came to anything.

That sort of unrest seemed to have gone on for a period of time. In the end the landlord kept the land but he was no longer a landlord as he was before the war.

He (the landlord) knew that we were not in Russia and that there was nothing in the law to suggest that. The uprising had to be brought down and without delay. The few who promoted the uprising were arrested and kept incarcerated until order was restored.

Then it seemed as if every day were a feast day in town. The local band was playing all day long going up and down the street and around the town, in the morning with the red flag, in the afternoon with the white one.

A day didn't go by without party political speeches in the public square where hundreds of people gathered to hear what the politicians had to say.

Leaders of the political parties more notably the Christian Democratic Party (D.C.P.) the Italian Communist Party (P.C.I.) the Italian Socialist Party (P.S.I.) the Movimento Sociale Italiano Party (M.S.I.) and the Monarchist Party who were telling the masses to rally behind the party of their choice and to be patient, the day would come, the day they had long been waiting for, the day of the return of the king, which never materialised.

But the people were hungry, they were tired of waiting and hearing promises, they wanted facts not words, they wanted jobs and not promises, and above all, they wanted food for their children. They were ready to listen to anybody who would promise to give work and food.

In the meantime foreign aid was coming through at a certain speed considering that at the time all the other countries had problems of their own too, one way or another. That seemed to appease the people and helped to carry on to the next stage.

Meanwhile, the Communist Party, the second largest party after the D.C.P, was preaching to the peasants that they would inherit the land they were cultivating. The Communists formed the first unions since they were abolished by Mussolini when he came to power, more than two decades earlier.

The M.S.I. was looking for another Mussolini. Its members were not convinced yet that the Fascists were the party of the nightmare, the party of the past, the party gone forever for most of the Italian people. Although they had a large number of young people behind them, there were not enough to impress anyone.

The Monarchist Party was seeking the return of Umberto II, the ex-king of Italy who abdicated and went into exile in Portugal after the invasion. They had the older people with them but there again not enough to speak of. Even the monarchy had passed into history.

But the D.C., being the favourite party abroad and at home, had secured a predominant role not only at government level but at regional and provincial level also. It secured the massive aid coming in from the allies' governments (mainly from the United States of America).

Citizens of the U.S.A. were bombarding Italy with parcels of all sorts and sizes. This contributed to the economy and of course in turn helped the people enormously. It gave a foothold to the leap Italy was about to take into a new future, into the unknown future which after a long wait turned out to be a relatively prosperous one.

In Serradifalco things were visibly different a year or two after the war, but being a small town things were not moving as fast as people wanted. In big cities things were different. The influx of tourists and investments from abroad was an enormous contribution to the development of the regions.

Massive aid came first, then the supporting propaganda needed to elect the first democratic government in a new republic. De Gasperi, a great statesman, one of the great politicians of modern time, was elected Prime Minister, the first of post war Italy. It was the beginning of a new era, an era much wanted by all the people of Italy.

De Gasperi was one of the founders of the E.E.C. One of the seven architects who masterminded what is today the strong front in Europe.

Although peace and order was restored reasonably soon, some pockets of lawlessness remained for some time.

Black marketeers flourished. They sprang up overnight, they had a free hand, they were dealing unhindered without any fear whatsoever. Money became worthless, it was losing its value faster than people could cope with. You needed a thousand lire a few months after the war to buy what you could buy for a few hundred lire a few months before. Inflation went up a thousand fold; it was eating into people's earnings unscrupulously. That was the worst thing that the war left behind.

Serradifalco is where I was born and brought up. It had a

population of seven thousand five hundred. It is located roughly in the centre of Sicily, in the province of Caltanissetta.

Sicily, an autonomous region of Italy, has nine provinces with a total population of five and half a million inhabitants. Its area is twenty six thousand square kilometres. The regional government is in the capital city of Palermo.

It was the wish of the people to have autonomy for the island, which has worked well up to the present time.

In the early fifties a rumour went around that a big firm from the north was coming to Serradifalco to test the underground surroundings for new minerals. In the summer of 1955 explorative drilling began.

After several months of work and enormous sums of money, money provided by the regional government, there was the good news of success. They found large deposits of potassium and other minerals. Work started immediately with the creation of many jobs.

For Serradifalco and the surrounding area it was a new era. Previously, the extraction of sulphur, which had been of value for many centuries, had claimed the lives of many. This was due to poor mining practices and lack of funding. Those days had left bad memories for everyone and they will be remembered for many years to come. A week didn't go by without a casualty and yet the people were against total abandonment.

They were against the big development, the rush to riches, for they knew big development brings destruction, big machines shorten the life of the underground deposit, and yet it had to be done, there was not much choice. In order to improve the condition of the industry it had to be done.

There was very little consultation at all between management and the workforce, decisions were unilateral, taken by the employers only. Sulphur was abandoned and preparations for complete mechanisation started. The labour force from the sulphur mines was gradually absorbed into the new industry.

The prospect of jobs was creating other jobs, not only for Serradifalco, but for many other towns around. The mines are in the territory of San Cataldo, a much larger town, thirteen kilometres from Serradifalco, but with the mines being only a short distance from Serradifalco, most of the business took place in my town. A year later the work force doubled.

The firm itself had brought in some people from the north of Italy where they had closed other mines and therefore some of the work force had to be relocated. The people from the continent, as we called them, had the right to come according to the firm's policy. They came with the machinery, machinery local people had never seen before, so apart from being necessary in order for them to keep their jobs, they helped to train the new employees.

The firm was Montecatini, one of the biggest employers in the country. It built the most modern establishment of the time. All machines and existing buildings were scrapped and new towers went up. A twenty kilometre Teleferica (aerial railway) was installed from Bosco-Palo (the mine's location) to Campo Franco where the raw material was to go to be refined. The hope of a job brought people back who had previously left and gone abroad.

I obtained work there, joining the installation team. The old machines were put aside making room for new ones. Derelict buildings were pulled down and replaced with new ones. Houses were built to accommodate the people from the north.

The team and I felt we were sowing the seeds for a big harvest. We thought we were putting up something to last for the next one hundred years, something to give sufficient work to the end of the century. In fact it was short lived, it was terminated after two decades.

Many farmers and farm workers left the land to join the industry. The artisans, who had a better chance because of the skill required, left their workshops to settle in the mine complex, where there was a better future and a better standard of living.

By the beginning of the sixties, prosperity was visible everywhere, money (which had regained some value after the fall in the years following the end of the war) was circulating more than anywhere else in the province. The industry expanded to neighbouring Campo Franco, Racalmuto and S. Cataldo.

"Compare" Ingnazio, who had left the land and had gone to France to work, had returned to take a job with Montecatini. He got in immediately with a good push from somebody well known, someone who could assure the administration that the man was a good worker.

That long ago if you had someone like a doctor, a priest, the mayor or a Member of Parliament that you could speak to, or a friend to speak for you, then there was a good chance of getting in. It is a way of assuring the employer that the man or woman is a good worker. This system is still there but on a smaller scale, of course.

At the time, unless people had a required skill and they could prove it, they needed support from one of above mentioned. Of course since then things have changed. Now it is mostly through application forms and other means of verifying that an applicant is who he says he is.

Farmers were doing well in Sicily and in the country as a whole right up to the mid-fifties, while farm labour was easily available and very poorly paid. Then it all changed. When the Americans flooded the market with cheap wheat and farm labour was getting expensive, many farmers had to abandon the farm and find an alternative.

Mpari, short for compare, is a noun we use when we are more

than friends or if there is a baptism, then the godfather becomes "compare", also the best man at a wedding and the groom are "compare", the wife is "commare". In Compare Ingnazio's case we were "compare" since we were very young and then we sealed it when he was married and I was the best man.

Compare Carmelo, like Compare Ingnazio, also left the land, and went to join his brother and family already in France, where he worked for a few years. He took a job in a machine shop where he was trained as a welder. He too, came back when the good news about Montecatini reached there. He got a job in the maintenance department, thanks to France for having given him some skills.

Compare Leonardo, like Compare Ingnazio and Compare Carmelo, was a farmer, one of those farmers who spends his life moaning and complaining that he could not make a living. He used to say that the price of the produce was not worth working for, or it rains too much, or it rains too little and so on and so forth.

He too tried to get in to Montecatini, but like many others who were unskilled he couldn't get a job. He didn't have the skills required and there were not enough unskilled jobs to hire all the inhabitants. He went to Germany and took a job with the Ford Motor Company, where he spent many years and managed to accumulate a small fortune.

My cousin Leonardo did so too. Leonardo was a builder, not a very happy builder, in fact when he went abroad and joined his brother Amedeo who was already in Germany, he changed his trade. He went to work for a manufacturing company where at first he appeared to be satisfied but soon he became disillusioned. Together with his brother he decided it would be a good idea to return to Italy and this they did.

They settled in Mantova in the north of Italy where Amedeo had been for twenty years before he had decided to move to Germany and they set up there permanently. Leonardo soon was married and built his own house.

Leonardo and I were very close when we were young, we were together every day after work, we spent hours of our youth making projects of all sorts, in the end we had to part company, it was very sad but it could not be helped. Eventually, one by one, more than half of our close friends left. In time some came back, some didn't.

The group was getting smaller and smaller, the outings were fewer and fewer, so were the tours and the picnics. The last party we had was in 1959 when going away was a novelty, at that age we thought leaving home was great, we felt that we were missing out, we thought anywhere else would be better. But was it?

Compare Cicciu went to Turin to work for FIAT, Colomba and Ensa went to America but unfortunately contact was lost after they departed. They were the first women I knew to leave home, it looked bad at the time. In the fifties it didn't look nice for a girl to go to work, but that was the changing times and there was no going back. Many people thought it was about time girls did something for a living.

In December 1960 I was informed that my appointment for an interview concerning my application to emigrate to Canada was on 15th January 1961 at the Canadian Embassy in Rome. On 13th January I caught the morning train to Rome.

This was my second time in Rome. I had taken my sister a few years earlier when she went for the same reason so I knew my way around. The interview at the Canadian Embassy went very well, a few questions to be answered, all very formal. The interviewer, who appeared to be a French-Canadian, went through the procedure telling me what I already knew since I had been there previously with my sister.

He said, "Canada welcomes you to a new land of opportunity."

I asked, "Are there any jobs?"

He hesitated, looked again through my papers and then said, "Yes, I would say for you it will be easy enough."

He gave me some leaflets with pictures of landscapes, towns and consumer goods and of course the permit and the visa.

He said, "Now it is up to you, you may leave whenever you like."

It was a cold January day, the sun was shining over the Eternal City. It was about 2 pm, I had had nothing to eat all day and yet was not hungry. It must have been the interview and the visa that made me realise what I was about to do. Anyway I found a room for the night, had a shower, went down for something to eat and then back up to bed.

The following morning I got up quite early, had breakfast, a good look around the city and then headed down to the station to catch the afternoon train.

I reached the station in good time, time enough for a cup of coffee and a biscuit. I sat at the bar overlooking the outside door; suddenly a young man coming towards me said, "Ciao."

I looked up not sure that this young man was addressing me. I paused for a few seconds and then said, "Do I know you?"

"Ha," he said, "I know you, A. Capritta isn't it? I'm Carmine."

The name rang a bell, "but it can't be" I said to myself. The Carmine I knew was always running barefoot and badly dressed, this Carmine was dressed expensively from top to toe. Of course many years had gone by and many things could happen in such a long time.

"Carmine Ansalone?" I asked.

"Yes", he replied, with the sense of humour he always had, "You must remember torturing my feet."

He still remembered how cruel I was (I thought to myself) stepping on his toes from behind and making him scream.

"Well," I said, "I didn't expect to see you here, in fact as far as I knew you were abroad. Anyway what are you doing here…this is an extraordinary coincidence."

I offered him a seat and asked him to join me in a drink. We ordered and started chatting about old things, new things, families, friends and many other things.

"I have been in Rome since I left Serradifalco," Carmine said, "precisely sixteen years. A few years ago the family went to Belgium. I stayed behind, I didn't think I could do any better than this."

"So what do you do for a living?" I asked.

"I'm a spy," he replied, with no hesitation at all.

"Ha, ha", I said to myself, "this man can't be anybody else but Carmine!"

I cast my mind back some fifteen years when I knew him as a shoeless boy, telling me that he had three pairs of shoes and a new suit for Sunday and I believed all that.

I thought that at the time running without shoes was fun. My mother never let me, and I couldn't understand why. Until one day, while we were playing, Carmine's father went by and said to the boy, "Carmine, go home and put your shoes on."

Carmine answered, "Yes father, in a minute."

Thirty minutes later his father went by again. He said to the boy, "When I return if you are still without shoes I will hit you".

The boy replied reluctantly, "I will go now father."

That day Carmine never came back, and I never saw Carmine with shoes. I concluded that there were no shoes. From that moment I understood why my mother had forbidden me to take my shoes off. It was shameful and dangerous. Of course some couldn't afford essentials, for many the war was still going on.

On another occasion a group of us were talking about war, soldiers, aeroplanes and so on.

I said, "My cousin's a sergeant in the police force".

Carmine replied, "My uncle was a general in the war."

Back in Rome:

"Who do you spy for?" I asked.

"I spy for Stalin, and you" he asked, "what are you doing here?"

"I have been appointed ambassador to Japan".

We laughed. He realised that he was not as good as he used to be. He explained that the job he had was something to do with the railway canteen. By that time my train was pulling in so I said "Goodbye", shook hands and left.

I decided to join my youngest sister and family already in Montreal. My sister went to Canada after she was married in 1957.

My family, all of them, were against my going. I noted a sudden change in my mother, my grandmother, my grandfather, my brothers and my eldest sister (who followed me after a few years, together with her husband and son).

At the time I was wondering what my father would have said. He was against emigrating, he liked the family to stay together. He had the experience of being away after spending some time in East Africa. Perhaps, if he were still alive I wouldn't have left. That was the feeling I had then, and still have now.

My father died in 1956 when he was fifty years old after a hernia operation. At the time Italy and in particular Sicily was still licking the wounds the war left, so I blame the death of my father on poor staff and old equipment. He was operated on in S. Cataldo, at the Maida hospital, a very old hospital, in fact it didn't last long after a new hospital was built and the Maida hospital was closed for good.

After a few days something went wrong, something that never should have happened with an operation of the sort. Evidently the staff at the hospital couldn't cope with it and he was transferred to Caltanissetta to the Favorita hospital where he received immediate attention, but it was too late.

Apparently my father had internal bleeding which could have been prevented if they had x-rayed him before the operation. They would have found he had an ulcer which was the cause of the bleeding. The operation itself went very well but the unexpected was very unfortunate, very sad for the family.

My friends too were against my decision to emigrate, they criticised it, they told me that I would have to go a long way to get a job like I already had. But all I had in mind was to go and see something different, stay one or two years and come back to the job I was about to leave.

It was not as easy as that.

On 14th March I boarded the Saturnia, the sister ship of the Vulcania, one of the largest ships of the "Tirrenia Line". We left Palermo at 11 a.m. For the next two days there was a lovely, friendly atmosphere, music, good food and the sea was very calm until we got to Portugal. When we left Portugal and entered the Atlantic the sea changed and so did the people.

All went quiet. After twenty-four hours of the Atlantic Sea most of the people had disappeared into their cabins. They were suffering from seasickness, more than I was.

I spent the rest of the time in the back of the ship living on fruit, going twice a day to the dining room and taking just fruit and rushing to the rear of the ship.

After nine days at sea we landed at Halifax, Nova Scotia. It felt so good to walk on solid ground. We soon recovered and the horrible crossing was soon forgotten, I lost quite a bit of weight on the journey which was an experience I had not expected.

We went through the customs check where I had to surrender two bottles of vermouth (a present for my sister) otherwise I had to pay more than they cost in the first place. That was my first upset. Then off we went, I and some friends I met on the ship. The first thing we did was to go and find a shop to buy some food and some cigarettes. Since I had said I knew some English, this was to be the test.

I found out that what I knew was not enough, I had to explain what I wanted using hand signs. That was disappointing and embarrassing. I excused myself, saying; "The English language in Canada, is not as easy as the English learnt in our schools." Eventually we got drinks, some sweets, and cigarettes. It was a nice day but it was cold, very cold for us.

There was snow everywhere, although the pavement was mostly under cover. There were some icy patches and because we were unprepared it was very difficult to walk on. So we went into a shop and bought some overshoes to be prepared for when we needed them. Overshoes in Canada are much needed, you cannot get anywhere without them. We went to find our luggage and got on the train which was waiting for us.

The train journey from Halifax to Montreal was very long and very tiring. It was a train for immigrants only. It was slow. It was stopped whenever there was another faster train going by. It seemed if it stopped forever, it seemed as if that train had nowhere to go, it gave the impression that it was transporting people with no fixed address, as if we were refugees looking for some place to have us.

The landscape at first was nice. We loved looking out of the window. It was fascinating. Most of us had never seen so much snow in our lives, except on television. Then it became boring. We were getting tired and anxious to get to our destination.

The train itself was not pleasant in any way. It didn't have the facilities of long distance trains. The crew, with their reticence for immigrants, did not help either. People were complaining about various things. The people in charge of the train gave an answer something like: "This train was prepared for you, to take you directly to your destination."

"Obviously this isn't the kind of train you see in films, on television or in booklets, with panoramic windows, big dining tables and the conductor helping the lady down the steps," I stated, "On the contrary this is a D.I.Y. train from A to Z."

The man became most annoyed when the chap next to me said, "We will file our complaint when we get to Montreal."

The man, apparently responsible for the train journey, evidently didn't like the fact that we didn't like the poor transport. He went away when he couldn't get a word in edgeways, to return later with somebody who could speak some Italian, but that didn't change the fact that the train was not adequate by any means.

We pointed out that the water was not up to standard. There was nothing clean to be seen and there was nowhere one could get food or drinks. Some people had filled their bags with food before they left the ship but many more had left the ship with nothing thinking that they could buy what they needed on the way.

The man replied through the interpreter that he was there to see the train get from Halifax to the various destinations and nothing else was of his concern. So the conclusion was that no one on the train knew who could answer our questions

A thousand miles and twenty-four hours later the train pulled into Windsor Station, Montreal. After I had put all my belongings together I, and many others, left the train. Most of the friends I had made on the eleven days' journey proceeded to Toronto and farther west.

Upstairs in the arrival hall there was my sister waiting anxiously with her husband and the children, among hundreds of others waiting for dozens of us. There was Michele Amico, a friend of my sister's family who gave me a hand with my luggage. Michele, who originally was from my home town although I didn't know him, was the owner of the house my sister was living in.

Michele lived on the first floor, my sister on the second floor. So the first friends I made were Signora Maria, Michele's wife, and Grace and Diana their daughters.

They were all very nice people. The following day I learned that Diana was expecting her fiancée from Italy any day. In fact he arrived a week after me. They were married three months after his arrival.

It was the first wedding I attended in Montreal; a marriage that went badly wrong. I gather that he didn't realise how far from his mother he was going. After a few weeks he got a job, a good job I would say, but he couldn't get used to the Canadian life. In fact after a few years he had had enough of it. He started talking about going back, leaving his wife and children. He did in fact go and never returned.

The last day of travelling was the longest. I felt tired, I felt lost and worried, I felt I wanted a bath and a good meal. I had lost 5 kg during the eleven days' journey. After a bath and a meal I felt almost new again, in the meantime I thought I was dreaming, I couldn't believe I had done this.

Later that evening friends and neighbours were coming in to say hello and to ask about their relatives. It is customary in my part of the country, when somebody arrives, to visit as soon as you can. So I met quite a lot of people that night, most of whom I had never seen in my life, some of whom hadn't moved one inch in the twenty or thirty years they had been in Canada. They were all good friends, it was like being at home talking about things and people asking me questions which mostly I couldn't answer.

The next morning, at 9 o'clock, I went out. I wanted see and explore Montreal. I went around a couple of blocks. It was like being in Italy, the whole street was lined with Italian shops. Everybody was speaking Italian. There was an Italian hall, an Italian church, a car dealer and a bakery and furthermore a dentist, an oculist and all sorts of professional places. Soon I realised that this was indeed the Italian part of Montreal! At the time there were four hundred thousand Italians in and around the city.

Although the sun was out and very bright, it was very cold. There was ice everywhere. I had my overshoes on, the ones I bought in Halifax, and yet my feet were freezing. I jumped on a bus that came along and travelled southwards on St. Lawrence Boulevard which runs from one end of the island to the other (north-south). I got off at Saint Catherine Street, also a very well-known street, which runs across (East-West). I started my walk westwards. It was the lunch hour and people were coming out of the offices, rushing in all directions.

I found myself rushing with them. No more slow walking, no more time for thinking, just looking where I was going. At home people do not rush like this I kept telling myself, people have more time, they take more time, they allow time for walking, for eating, for talking, even for looking around. It was really mad. It was really cold. It was strange but that was understandable and I liked it. For the time being anyway.

Now a job comes first, I said to myself. Jobs were scarce, especially at that time of the year March when I arrived). Usually in the winter months it is hard to find jobs as many firms reduce the workforce at the beginning of the winter when work slows down. But, as we say, if you've got friends, you've got no problems.

Two days later a friend came to tell me there was a job going at Pontvieu foundry where he had worked for the past three years. Was I interested? I had no idea what the job was like or what sort of place it was. He explained but I still didn't know what it was about, what a foundry was like. We left it that I would meet him in the morning.

Pontvieu Foundry was about one and a half miles from where my sister lived. The foundry itself was a French-Canadian enterprise, but the workforce of about fifty was from all over Europe and beyond. It was a dusty, hot, heavy-working place. Not my line of work at all but it was a start!

Two weeks went by, and another job came along, this time more to my liking. "Barzel Art Metal", the name of the establishment, was a small place with twenty-five working on the floor, nineteen of whom were Greeks, two Hungarian, one from Egypt, one French-Canadian and one other Italian and me. There were three part-time in the office - one English-Canadian, one French-Canadian and one Italian lady.

There were also three permanent people working in the office: the accountant, English-Canadian, a secretary, French-Canadian and the girl at the switchboard whose nationality I never knew.
Mr. Mandel, the owner, was a Jewish man from Europe. He had moved to Canada after the war, and was very good at running his business. In the morning he was first to arrive. There was also a foreman. He would go around the shop all day with a piece of bread in one hand and a cup of coffee in the other.

The factory made ornamental iron furniture, very modern furniture produced in large quantities and shipped all around the country. Mandel was the proprietor of the factory and his wife the manager. There were ten salesmen, one in each province. The products were promoted in showrooms in all the provinces.

The company was well established in Verdon, a suburb of Montreal. It took me sixty minutes to get there by bus, very inconvenient and uncomfortable. It wouldn't have been so bad if it was only one bus, but to change three times annoyed me very much especially in winter when one had to wait sometimes fifteen or twenty minutes in the freezing cold, so it was not for me.

A car was really the answer. In fact soon I managed to get one and that made life easier. I could sleep a bit longer in the morning, I got to work in good time and in the evening got home half an hour earlier. At work things were proceeding in a satisfactory way but I had to be content at first, the pay was very little. After two weeks I asked for more money and got it without a fuss.

Four weeks later I asked Mr. Mandel again, this time for a higher increase, for I knew he couldn't afford to let me go. Jumping to his feet and getting rather agitated he said, "Out of the question!" After a slight pause he calmed down and was looking at a piece of paper on the desk.

"Really, the firm cannot afford it," he said.

"Well, Mr. Mandel, if the firm can't afford it I'll have to look for another job", I pointed out.

In the next pay packet I found the money I wanted!

The weekend after I arrived, Dino, a friend of the family, came to see me. He had been in Montreal for five years already, so he knew where to spend a few hours when we went out. After that we went out regularly every weekend for some years. Dino always tried to distract me, for I was sad at times thinking of the family and friends I had left behind. It didn't take me long to realise the mistake I had made going abroad.

Although my sister and family were a very good help, I missed the family on the other side of the Atlantic. I was worried for my mother who was still in pain after the loss of my father. I was concerned for my brother Pino, who was in the army. He had joined for his compulsory service in the army for eighteen months after graduating.

In Italy it is compulsory to serve in the army, the navy or the air force for eighteen months. This left my brother Enzo, the youngest of the family, in his last two years before graduation.

After my father died, being the oldest in the family, I felt a sense of responsibility.

In the part of the country where I came from there is a customary sense of duty, it is the way we are brought up. When the head of the family dies the oldest male heir inherits the responsibility to look after the family. It is a natural duty.

I had left neither romance nor sweethearts behind, just family and friends. One evening when I got home I found my mother's first letter. It read, "Dear son, thank you for your letter received this afternoon. I'm pleased to hear that you had a good journey and that you found everybody well. Here is as you left it, we still can't get used to the idea that you are no longer with us. We wish you all the best and may god bless you. Love from all of us. Your mother."

My mother felt very much let down when I left, they all felt let down, my mother, my maternal grandfather, grandmother and sister. They wondered what had got into me. At the time I didn't calculate the implications, the bitter taste and the pains I left in my family life, I deserted them when they needed me most. I didn't realise that until it was too late. It was a mistake that has tormented me all my life.

Without delay, I answered the same day.

"Dear mother, I don't want you to worry about me, I'm all right, we all are. Soon my two years here will be over. I've seen the City and I think it is very nice, so are the people.

I had a lot of visitors when I arrived, all of them very friendly. Yes, the job is what I wanted. Don't worry, this is a big place, there are a lot of jobs, so it would be unthinkable for me to accept a job unless it was in my line of work."

A few months later I met Tony Bisecco, then Enzo Lomando. At that time, Tony was an amateur music writer. Enzo was an amateur singer and I an amateur songwriter. We made up a trio and soon we made the first record, then another. The songs were in Italian, the market was not large enough for profit making, which we knew, so we did it for fun, for pleasure.

The first song, "Una Stretta di Mano" (a handshake), I wrote for a certain person.

For Tony, Enzo and me singing and writing were just hobbies but the recording was done professionally at R.C.A. Victor studio in Montreal, with six professional musicians including the Maestro Arturo Romano, well known in the field of music, who also arranged the songs.

We called the company "A.R.C.O.". Tony later formed a group, a small orchestra, only to play at weddings, parties and occasions of that kind. The friendship went on but we never made another recording.

Enzo was singing with various groups in the Montreal area. We often met, the three of us discussing over a cup of coffee or over a walk in the park about a possible recording, the conclusion was, it would be too expensive, the market for an Italian recording was not there so we put the matter to rest for good.

In May that year, after I had been to New York, visiting relatives, friends and of course Broadway and part of the great City itself, I wanted to see Toronto, Niagara Falls and part of Ontario.

New York was so busy, it was a fast moving City. I saw people eating their lunch on the run as if someone was chasing them, extraordinary, something I had never seen before. One of my relatives remarked, "This is New York life."

A few weeks after I resumed work, I asked John if he would be interested in coming for a weekend in Toronto.

"Oh yes, I've wanted to do that for a very long time," he said.

John was the Egyptian I mentioned earlier who was working with me at Barzel's.

On a Friday after work at 4 pm we started the 355 mile journey from Montreal to Toronto. It was a lovely May afternoon, the sun was still high and hot, as hot and humid as it could be in the summer, that is around 90 degrees F.

Just before we got onto the highway, we saw a girl on the verge, apparently looking for a lift.

"Shall we take her?" I said.

"It might be trouble," John answered.

Anyway, I stopped. She asked for a lift.

I said a bit hesitantly, "Get in."

She said, "Oh…there is my friend too."

She pointed to a young man on the other side of the road. Obviously they were looking for a lift in either direction. I looked carefully, they seemed all right to me, so "Get in," I said again and off we went.

"Where are you going?" I asked.

"Oh as far as you can take us," the girl replied.

It was a very nice afternoon and we had four hours of sunshine in front of us. Once on the highway it was 90 mph all the way. In the summer at ten o'clock at night the sun is still visible and quite hot. The girl, whom I was keeping an eye on through the mirror, was of medium build, about five feet five, blond with hard features. She had short hair, long dangling earrings and dark glasses. She was wearing a flowered blouse with a rather low open neck and jeans. The young man was slightly taller, with curly brown hair and slim. He was wearing a Hawaiian shirt, jeans and sandals. Both of them were carrying a coat over their arm.

After a few miles on the 401 highway the girl was becoming impatient and restless, her expression changed, her mood was not the same. It seemed to me as if at any moment she was going to ask me to stop the car so that she could jump out.

The young man was more relaxed, he kept telling her: "Reste tranquille," (French for "stay calm").   I felt   somehow uncomfortable. John's remarks were coming back to me. I didn't know what to do…. Suddenly an idea came to my mind. "When we get into Ontario we might meet a friend of mine. I met him some time ago," I said.

"Who is he?" John asked.

"A policeman," I answered.

The man in the back looked at the girl as if to say, what are we going to do. After a few miles I stopped at a petrol station. Still part of my trick, I said to John who was more worried than I was, "Pretend to be asleep while I go to pay."

When I came back the couple were gone.

"They left very smoothly without a word, they just left," John whispered.

"My trick worked," I murmured.

"What trick?" my companion asked.

"The trick about the policeman," I continued.

"They didn't say why they left or if they were coming back."

I felt relieved, I felt quite satisfied that my trick had worked and that I had got them out as quickly as I got them in.

I drove up to Cornwall, Ontario, where I pulled up for a drink at a motorway restaurant. There we found the police checking all cars going by.

It was not the policeman from my joke.

"What is going on officer?" I asked.

"Oh, we are just making sure everything is all right and the cars are clean inside and out," the officer replied.

After a brief pause and a drink we continued our journey.

We stopped for the night in Toronto. On Saturday morning while visiting the Metropolis, John spotted in the newspaper, "The Toronto Star", a headline which read: "The police are looking for a couple connected with a burglary in Montreal." The man and the woman fitted the description and location of my passengers.

In the afternoon we drove to Niagara. The waterfalls were very impressive. St. Catherine itself, the adjoining town, is an extraordinary place, full of life, with a lot to see and a lot to do.

We went to the top of the tower where one can see both sides of the border as far as one's sight can reach. It was absolutely breath-taking, far exceeding what you see on television or in a film. The number of tourists pouring in and out at that time of the year was as you would imagine. And there we were looking at something we didn't expect, a marvel that took us a long time to get over.

We stayed in St. Catherine for the night. After we had booked into a motel we went out to have dinner and then a drink in a night club, it was very inviting but we had to go and have some sleep and prepare for an early start.

On Sunday morning we crossed into the United States of America, where we had breakfast in a café in Buffalo. Buffalo is a good size town, an old town I would say, especially down town where we could see old wooden houses abandoned and left to rot.

By noon we were on the way back to Montreal.

Driving along, just for the sake of a chat I asked John, "What were the circumstances that brought you to Canada, John?"

"Politics, politics and economics, were the circumstances," he replied. "Politically, we were cut off completely when the world withdrew its support, economically ruined. When the Pharaoh went, all his people went down with him. In 1952 the Pharaoh was dethroned and forced out of the country leaving behind Maj. Gen. Mohammed Naguib, President and Premier of Egypt. In 1954, having defeated Gen. Mohammed, Gamal Abdel Nasser came to power, his regime didn't like us and we didn't like the regime."

"My father," John explained, "was a personal tailor to the Pharaoh, the King of Egypt, in particular he made his shirts. The Pharaoh was particularly fussy about his shirts, he wanted them nicely fitted and properly done. We couldn't understand why, but he only wore the shirts once. My father was working full time for the palace you know. So when Nasser took over, my father found himself without a job and without a country for that matter. So we decided to leave the country we all loved very much and start life somewhere else once again."

Going further back in time John went on, "We are Armenians you know, we had to leave Armenia for the same reasons. I didn't want to leave Egypt, at least until I finished my schooling."

John was educated at an Italian Catholic school in Cairo where he learned Italian, French and English. He had two more years to go to obtain a sort of certificate.

Now John was attending night courses at McGill University in Montreal, hoping that in a few years he could get a better job than at Barzel's.

"Do you feel somehow as if you have been castigated by Nasser, because you and your family were too close to the Pharaoh or just because you were an admirer," I asked.

"Yes, I do feel castigated. Almost overnight we went from being efficient to inefficient. Our future looked very bleak, even our friends distanced us, for fear of being seen with us. We couldn't take money or clothes with us out of the country, except the allowances that meant the ticket one way out and the clothes we had on. It didn't look good but that was it, take it or leave it."

"We had a lot of friends before all this happened, most of them turned their back on us but a few remained loyal. By trusting a few faithful friends we got clothes and money out of the country with their help, after we paid a certain amount of money. We had to pay to take what we wanted with us through the black market."

"Tell me about the Pharaoh, John," I asked, interrupting, when I saw he was getting too emotional.

"Oh yes," he answered rather pleased, "he was a very good man, he treated us as if we were part of his family. He had some extraordinary eating habits you know. He liked pigeons, he liked to breed them for food. His breakfast consisted of a dozen pigeon eggs and a cupful of pigeon broth. The eggs were fried, the broth made out of six young pigeons boiled for some hours to obtain a concentrated liquid then left to cool to lukewarm before he drank right from the cup. He said that this sort of diet kept him fit."

"Was he fit, John?" I asked.

"If that is what he called fit, yes. I myself would say it was rather something out of proportion, a bit wasteful. Mind you he was keeping the pigeon population down and he insisted on that. He used to say that that sort of diet gave him the feeling of being

146

the only person who could do it, and that was great."

John said, "The Pharaoh, in the last years of his rule, did not have as many admirers as he used to. He was becoming less and less popular. He could see that the era of the Kings was passing into history. He could see as well how fast the world was changing and how the people were getting more resentful day by day."

"Do you think that if he had changed his attitude, his way of doing things, his policies and gave up some powers he would have survived, I mean could he have appeased his adversaries? I suggested.

"Perhaps for another six months or a year." John replied." His admirers were getting fewer and fewer, everybody knew that the end was inevitable from all points of view. But we never thought his regime would deteriorate so quickly. But then when you pursue one policy you never know what the other party is planning."

"In the early fifties," John continued, "disorder started, in Cairo the capital, in particular, anti-government cells developed, and soon after turmoil was evident all over the country. People were growing dissatisfied with the monarchy, they had had enough of the Pharaoh. For me that was predictable but I didn't think it would happen so soon.

Of course there was a lot of optimism in and around the palace.

We didn't have any idea of how fast things were fermenting, how hungry the people were for power. It was like a ticking bomb which was going to explode under your seat and you couldn't do anything."

As we continued our journey there was a long pause while we enjoyed the scenery we were passing through, the landscape, the vast fields on both sides of the highway rising smoothly to hills, then to mountains and then to higher peaks, the flat green fields, the thick woods after that and still farther, the remaining snow covering the peak tops. The traffic in both directions was incomparable with the traffic on the European roads.

On the roads through the sparsely populated areas it was a pleasure for motorists to drive, easily keeping their distance and contemplating what nature has to offer in that part of the world, allowing themselves to relax and think. "God planted the woods where people are cold," I remarked suddenly, referring to fuel.

"What was that?" John asked.

"I believe trees grow where needed most. You haven't got woods in Egypt, John, have you, nor in many hot countries for that matter. Here in North America fire is life, like in hot countries food is existence," I pointed out.

"Are there woods in Sicily, Angelo?" John interrupted.

"Yes there are, high in the mountains, where winter can be very cold. Here in Canada trees are everywhere. So are the cold winters."

John took time to reflect on what I had said and then replied, "You know, in Egypt people can go without food for a while, but here I don't think we could go without heat for long."

For a minute or two there was silence, a long pause…then, "You haven't said what brought you here yet, have you?" John asked.

I didn't know what to say, he really caught me off guard, I didn't expect that, not just then, not while we were talking about him but I was glad it was nothing like the reason that had brought him to Canada.

"Just for the experience, I came here to see North America, therefore I make myself believe that in two years I'll be back home and able to tell my friends and my family about the North Americans, their habits, their land and their weather. So I'll try to see as much of the country as I can."

"Perhaps you'll change your mind after the first winter in Montreal. I wanted to go back after the first winter but I had to give more time, for I have all my family here. We have some property in Egypt you know, to which we lose our rights after ten years, but I don't think we could cope with Nasser and his rigid regime."

John, changing the subject said, "You are doing well with Barzel, are you not? It seems to me as if he (Barzel I mean) likes you."

"He likes my work you mean. I don't think the man likes me more than he likes anybody else."

We pulled off near Kingston (Ontario). I stopped at a lay-by to have a drink. I got the flask out and two cups and poured it out. I noticed that the drink was cold.

"There must be something wrong with my flask." I said.

John had a sip and… "Your coffee is coca cola!"

We laughed. The hotelier whom I had asked to fill the flask must have misunderstood me.

This was a mistake I made often, when I asked for a coffee I got Coca-Cola instead. I realised after a while where the confusion was. I was not opening my mouth enough!

After a short rest we continued our journey arriving in Montreal at 8 pm quite pleased with our outing.

We were tired but satisfied with what we had seen during the weekend. The first thing we noticed when we got in the centre of city was the difference between the two cities. Toronto after working hours, and especially at weekends, is a very quiet city, whereas Montreal is very much alive all the time.

The next few months really were routine, up at 7 a.m. to start work at 8, finish at 5 p.m. go home, have something to eat and out for the usual walk, one of my habits which I never lost. I often went down to Jarry Park where one meets people of all sorts, colours and creeds.

Jarry Park is a large area with many sporting activities. It is in the middle of a large European community, therefore apart from the North American sports there were European sports too, including soccer where anybody could join in. There I sat, watching people coming in and people going out, people shouting, laughing doing all sorts of things, reminding me of my town and my friends, bringing back memories of Serradifalco.

Sitting on a wooden bench with my back to the sun on my own, my mind went blank, my sight blurred, the voices of all those people around me seemed to get farther and farther away, I felt as if I fell asleep with my eyes open. I was very far away, as far as the mind can get, wondering how my mother was coping in my absence, if Enzo (my brother) had done his exams and how Pino (my other brother) was getting on with his promotion. When I left, Pino was on a course to be an army officer. I was also anxious to know how the place I'd left in the making (the mining complex) was progressing.

After six months in Montreal, I had met French, Greeks, and Spanish, people from Poland, England and of most European origins. I had met people from the East, the Middle East, from the continent of Africa, South America, from all over the world.

151

In Montreal it is possible that in a place where one works there could be as many as 20-30 nationalities so you may be dealing with many different cultures, different people and different languages, many confusing languages, every day. But the language I wanted to learn was English but I was not making much progress. One may learn bits and pieces of many languages but to learn one properly is not easy without attending language classes.

I had to learn some Greek, to communicate with personnel in Barzel's workshop when I was put in charge since the workforce was mostly Greek. I called them "people from the boat". Barzel's was their first job. They were brought in as soon as they came off the boat, by friends or relatives. They were very poorly paid with no security whatsoever.

At the time unions were virtually non-existent, security of employment was at the employer's discretion. Many of them, after months or perhaps years, found another job and left, but some stayed for years for lack of language or initiative. The men were unskilled and didn't have much to give except goodwill. What they were learning at Barzel's was not much to rely on, it was very basic and not enough to find another job easily.

Although my mother wrote often and I answered as quickly as I could, the letters were more or less all the same. But from time to time there was some good news. The next letter was full of good things.

"Dear son," one read, "I'm glad to hear that you met your uncle, aunt and cousins. They were very pleased to have met you and they look forward to seeing you again. Pino has been promoted to lieutenant. He will get his leave shortly. Enzo passed his exams.

Grandfather tells me that the farm produce this year is average. The fruit is good, the almonds, walnuts and pistachios are not so good. But for the grapes and the olives they are predicting a good harvest.

Often I meet friends. They ask after you and send their regards.

Love for you all, your mother."

We were all very pleased with the news, my sister and her husband and me.

My mother kept me well informed of everything. She knew that I loved the farm and all what was there. I enjoyed every bit of time I spent there.

The farm is a small one, a very productive piece of land. Almost everything that grows in Sicily grows there. I loved the place. I used to go almost every day for one hour or two, sometimes to help my grandfather and sometime for pleasure. It was a mile from town, a perfect walking distance.

Sometimes I went twice, especially in the summer months when my grandparents were staying at the cottage, for the summer harvest. I enjoyed the heat of the day and nice evenings, sitting outside with the silver moon shining overhead lighting the surrounding hills, listening to the crickets and watching the bats flying in the silence of the night while my grandparents were preparing for the next morning.

When my grandfather died, my mother took on the management of the farm. Unfortunately, none of us took that line of work. The farm then became uneconomical, since my mother had to pay to have the work done. Farm labour had become scarce, it was getting more and more expensive every day, so my mother decided to maintain what she could and leave the rest uncultivated.

In November 1961 came the first snowfall of my first winter in Montreal. The first snow is stormy, ferocious, very heavy and comes to everybody's surprise. It caught everyone unprepared. A few feet of snow could accumulate in a few hours. For people driving the chances are that they will walk home once their cars stop due to the bad weather. Goods vehicles and heavy cars make the journey with difficulty, but they make it. Perhaps it will be a long journey but they get home. The older and lighter cars have no chance. So they are pushed to the kerb and left to be collected when the snow is cleared. The first of the bad weather catches almost everybody without proper footwear, without adequate clothing and most importantly the cars still with summer tyres. In Canada and I would think anywhere where the snow is in abundance, people change to snow tyres in winter.

If near home people walk, otherwise they try to catch the bus just to keep warm, if they are lucky enough to find a space, the buses get so crowded. Snowmobiles come out as soon as there is enough snow to run on. Very effective machines in the snow, they are used by the police to get quickly to accidents and hold-ups, which are frequent in Montreal, and by the hospital emergency services to ferry emergency cases to hospital.

If it snowed overnight, in the morning people would awake to the very undesirable and inconvenient job of digging the car out which could take hours. If they remembered where they left it!

I remember more than once getting up in the morning and seeing everything covered up. I took my shovel and found neighbours trying to establish where they had left their cars. The snow was frozen hard, the temperature 15-20 degrees below freezing, but we had to dig the cars out if we wanted to get to work.

The City snow removers are efficient. They've got the machines they need. As soon as the snow starts falling the machines come out to clear the roads. It is fascinating to watch them at work. Snow combines I called them, because they are like the combines the farmers use. They have a huge vacuum in the front, behind the rotating blades, sucking in the snow by the tonne and blowing it out through the offside where a lorry runs parallel with the combine. The lorry fills up in minutes then takes it to the nearest park or outskirts of the city to be piled up where it will stay until late spring waiting for the warm sun to melt it away.

On the whole, the snow annoys everybody, but it also gives enjoyment to many. We enjoyed going out after the snowfall especially if it occurred at the weekend. With the excuse of helping the children with the sledge I used to have a ride or two.

The snow gives employment to thousands for months. It is hard work but it pays well.

Christmas festivities. The rush to buy Christmas cards, Christmas trees, Christmas presents, Christmas telephone calls and special items for special dinners.

Not only do the poor get poorer, as they say, by spending what they have saved through the year, but people also take time off work for Christmas shopping and then on the top of that lose sleep thinking what to get for whom. I detested all that, to me it was absurd. I know that Christmas comes once a year and I agree that everybody should get into the spirit of the festivities but that some people should go over the top, to me it was a bit too much.

Although I consider the drinks and food at this time of the year can be wasteful, I enjoy the special food prepared with more time, with more detail, with more ingredients and with more people preparing it, that is to say a family celebration. Although I'm not a drinker I enjoy the odd drink such as Asti Spumante and some liqueurs that come out once a year for the occasion.

A few days before Christmas, I received a surprise letter from a friend I had made on the boat who went to Vancouver. He followed his fiancée who went a year earlier. "Dear A," he wrote, he addressed me by the initial - this was one of his ideas. When we were on the boat he said, "We are going to North America, you know. We must chew and call each other by the initial now. "He was chewing and calling friends by the initial long before we got there. He was very enthusiastic and a good natured young man, one of those jovial types.

"First of all I must apologise for not writing sooner," and he explained, "I had problems finding a job, problems with the language and then as if that was not enough, more problems fitting in. My fiancée has really grown up but she has grown in a different way. The ideas she had before she left Italy have all been forgotten. She told me, "Things have changed and so have we, we must allow ourselves more time." I told her that she was acting silly and unfair and that the new life in this New World has gone to her head. As you know I only have three months left and I do not know what to do."

Fernando (the friend in question) had three months left out of the one year he was allowed for marriage purposes, but if he could find an employer who would guarantee him work then he could stay.

"At present I have a job, not much of a job but it's a start," Fernando went on. "I already regret this adventure, this unnecessary upset but I'm here and it would be a shame not to stay at least for a few more years. You must be wondering why I'm telling all this to you. Well I felt I had to tell someone somehow, so I thought of you."

I met Fernando a day after I boarded the ship to Canada. I started my journey in Palermo and he started his in Naples. He told me a lot about his fiancée, he told me they had known each other as long as he could remember. I could understand his present anger. I knew well the place where he came from and I also know that he left a good job to be with the love of his life. Fernando came from a small town near Sorrento in the province of Naples where it never snows and never is cold. He recognised the mistake he had made sooner than I did but as they say when you are in the water you must swim and he had a lot of swimming to do.

I answered his letter without delay.

"Dear F. Thank you for having thought of me in circumstances like this. Undoubtedly that was a silly thing for your fiancée to do and irresponsible. However, I don't know what the circumstances are that changed your fiancée's mind. But I know you and I don't think that it was you who made her change mind. Nevertheless things happen. My advice to you is stick to your job, F. for a few more months and you will secure your stay in Canada." I never heard a word from him again.

Twelve months had already gone by since I arrived in Canada, the longest twelve months of my life. I had seen the spring go by, the days lengthening, stretching to the warming sun of the late spring, melting the great piles of snow which had accumulated through the winter months. Through the springtime I had seen the cold, the rain, the sunshine and the occasional light snowstorm. I went through the vernal heavy stormy weather with temperatures below twenty or even colder. I had seen the soft breeze of the late spring brushing away the remains of the last snowfall from the top of the pine trees.

The summer in Montreal at first is pleasant but then the temperature gets too high. Towards the middle of July it gets unbearable, a sticky heat, extremely humid. Generally, from the middle of July to the middle of August one can expect this sort of airless weather. There is little difference in the temperature between night and day.

This weather occurs for approximately four weeks between those two months (July and August). Each week the weather alternates. One week it is very hot and sultry. The following week there can be heavy thunderstorms which take place mostly in the night. Afterwards the weather is very nice and fresh smelling. In two or three days the temperature rises yet again to give another week of hot, damp and airless weather and so on.

As a whole the summers are very pleasant with plenty of sunshine. People go out to the countryside and to the beach. They go out most weekends picnicking, bathing and visiting places.

Montreal has many beautiful historic buildings, many religious institutions with a moving history built on a delightful landscape. It is a lovely city to visit in the summer months.

The largest and nearest body of water is Lake Champlain, forty-five miles from Montreal just across the US border, in the state of New York. This is a favourite place for bathing.

In the centre of Montreal there is a sanctuary, St. Joseph's Oratory, which is situated on Mount Royal. Mount Royal is 869 feet above sea level, overlooking the City. There is a lookout station near the top where visitors can go and look over the entire City and see St Helen's Island in the St Lawrence River. In 1967 the trade fair "EXPO 67" took place on the Island bringing much trade and many visitors to the city.

There are many churches in Montreal (as Aaron Mantel, the boss of Barzel said to me once, "There are more churches in Quebec than there are in Rome."). There are large churches and smaller ones, old and modern. Saint James' Cathedral was built to resemble Saint Peter's in Rome. It has many similarities but of course is nowhere near the size of Saint Peter's.

Saint Joseph's Oratory on Mount Royal is a very well-known place. People come from all over the United States and Canada in pilgrimage to the famous Sanctuary. Every time we had visitors, the first thing we did was to take them there. Montrealers go up to Mount Royal regularly whether for a walk, a picnic or just to have a seat in the sun. There is a well-maintained park with many walks and picnic areas.

There is a lake half way up, where birds, (water birds such as swans, ducks and similar) are kept through the summer months, an attraction for children and for all. In the winter months when the lake is frozen solid it is used for skating. There are also skiing activities on the mountain. A bar restaurant nearby provides hot and cold food and drinks all year around.

Autumn is notable for a day by day change in the weather and in nature. The leaves of the maple tree (symbol of Canada), in particular, change from a dark green to a lovely gold and red and then to a pallid yellow before the wind shakes them to the ground. Rainfall is more frequent and the temperature drops to a considerably chilly one and continues steadily downwards to freezing point by the end of October when snowfalls are due to start. The winter months are long and cold stretching from the middle of October to the middle of April.

Two years had now gone by. I had established myself in my job and in Montreal's daily life. I had made a lot of friends. I was getting used to the idea that I was a foreigner and to unfriendly looks from Canadians. Many of the French Canadians were reluctant to speak to or associate with foreigners.

I had got used to the services such as shopping, transport, banking, offices, etc. I had lost some habits but retained some. I had to give up going out meeting friends every day as I did back home. I gave up going to the movies once a week and sometimes twice. I retained my daily walk, my daily espresso coffee and occasional cappuccino.

Queuing up was one of the things I didn't like. We had to queue at the banks, at shops, at the bus stop, at the cinemas and even at the restaurants. I was used to none of this. It reminded me of back home in the late forties when people had to queue for food and goods with coupons. I didn't like it and I still don't like it but I had to queue as long as the others did.

The idea of going back after two years was fading. I could not make my mind up. I was hoping like all the others, the hope everybody had, the hope of a new country, the hope in the land of opportunity, where something might come along and make a fortune overnight. Really, I never believed in overnight fortunes, I relied on my skill and that was enough fortune for me.

I had promised nothing to anybody, only to myself. I had no obligation to anyone but to myself. On the other hand there was my mother, brothers and friends in Sicily whom I didn't want to lose either. I decided to give it more time.

In the spring of 1963 my sister Concettina, her husband Salvatore and their son Aldo came to Montreal. After four weeks they decided that Canada was not for them.

Having compared the job Salvatore was offered in Montreal and the job he had left, he thought he would be better off returning to Serradifalco. The work he had left at home was far better than he was offered in Montreal. Perhaps he should have given more time and thought to it but he, his wife and son returned to Sicily. But it didn't work as they expected. On his arrival back home he enquired after the job he had left but his place had been filled. So after a few months they decided to pack up again and go back to Canada.

Once more in Montreal Salvatore soon found work. After a while my sister also found work and so they established themselves for some time to come. Now they have an average home in an average part of Montreal, with an average standard of living. My nephew Aldo obtained a degree at McGill University. In 1965, after seven years in Canada, my younger sister Maria, her husband and their children, Salvatore and Felicia, returned to Italy with the firm intention of staying there for good. In fact soon after they arrived back they bought a house and a shop, starting trade almost immediately.

Two months later I decided to take four weeks' holiday. I thought after four years it was time I went to see my family and have a look around.

At home, I found everybody well. I received a great welcome from everyone. I felt a bit of a stranger for the first few days, even the people I knew looked at me as if I was a stranger. After four years I had to adjust myself to the changes I found. There had been enormous changes during the years I was away.

A sudden change in the economy modified the town enormously.

I could not understand how in such a short time things had upgraded so quickly. Even the landscape was modified, the people looked happier, the young had the best of it and the change in the economy meant more money in their pockets.

For the people of Serradifalco a month is a long time, they would want to know where one has been and what had happened. (Mind you when somebody leaves the town, immediately the news spreads by word of mouth.)

As a whole it looked a different picture. Construction of a higher standard was in full operation. New houses were being built, old houses under repair. People looked different to me, smarter for one thing. A man who was on foot before I left now had a bicycle; the man who had a bicycle now had a scooter; and the man who had a scooter now had a car. The man who had a small and older car now had changed it for a bigger and newer one.

The farmer who for centuries had cultivated the land by the old method (using mules, horses and donkeys) now had a tractor, had changed his working hours, increased his livestock and travelled by car. I was really taken by that and I'm very happy for them.

Was it the mining complex that had brought all this wealth? Was it Montecatini which had woken up the industry in Serradifalco? Was there another choice if Montecatini was not first? Or was it the evolution of the fifties and sixties?

The farmers and farm workers, the ones who were left, were now coming forward, they were seeking their share. The farmers had replaced the donkey, the mule, the ox and the horse with modern machinery. These animals, which were the main resource for working the land up to the fifties, had virtually disappeared by the middle of the sixties. Of course I'm talking about some parts of Sicily. Mainland Italy was already mechanised since the industrial revolution at international level.

In Sicily 75% of the farmland is on the hills making it very difficult to cultivate but, with the coming of the large bulldozers, it was possible to change the natural shape of the land. The hills have been flattened skilfully giving access to tractors of all sizes to climb and cultivate where, for thousands of years, only donkeys, mules, horses and oxen had gone.

Now, as far as one could see, the flattened hills were covered with vineyards and olive and fruit groves. It had improved the quality of work and the quality of life for the farmer. Without this technology it would have been impossible to cultivate those hills. It has given rise to a considerably better standard of living for the big farmer in general and the small farmer in particular.

I felt part of all this, for I had helped to plant the seeds which now bear fruit. The industry was in full swing now, the people were benefiting and I was glad to have had helped. The name Montecatini for some reason has been changed, perhaps for political or economic reasons to Montedison. Montecatini merged with Edison, another firm in the same line of business. Consequently, following the merger, Edison brought more people from the north and that caused a cut in the local workforce. This suggests that the partnership was more for economic reasons than politics.

Now Montedison was engaged in a petro-chemical development at Gela on the south cost of Sicily, about forty km from Serradifalco. It was expected to employ people from Serradifalco. This was good news for the younger generation. My compare Ingnazio was happy with what he was doing, as was compare Carmelo and many other friends. So there was progress, the expansion was visible, happy days ahead for everyone.

One day Padre Zoda (the parish priest) invited me for a chat. He never forgot the friendly arguments we had in the years before I left, arguments he always won. He was very pleased to see me after four years of absence. The first thing he said was, "You have not changed a bit in all this time. You look as you did the day before you left." He was very interested and wanted to know how my time abroad had been. He not only wanted to know about me but also about the "paesani," people from our town who went to Montreal before and after.

"First of all," he said, "tell me about yourself, places you have been to, the work you did and how long you will be staying or if you going back at all."

"Well," I answered modestly, "I don't think there is much to tell, it has not been all holiday you know, nevertheless I have been to one or two places. I've been working all the time and making the most of it, having some holidays, visiting places, some good and some not so good. My priority has been making friends and battling with the language. The job I got is in line with the work I had before I left -ornamental iron work."

"Have you been to New York?" he asked excitedly.

"Yes I have."

"Whereabouts?" he impatiently interrupted. (Impatiently because he couldn't wait to tell me that he had been there too.)

"I went to see the United Nations building, Forty-second Street, Broadway and…"

"Me too," interrupting again he said, "I had a tour of the UN building and a walk down Forty-second Street but I didn't go to a Broadway Theatre."

"You wouldn't, it wouldn't be appropriate for you."

I went back in time, back to the fifties when he was running the Cinema Parrocchiale, the Parish Cinema. He was very busy at the time cutting pieces out of the films, pieces he didn't want people to see, to the extent of not making any sense out of it.

"Angelo, it seems as if you forgot what you were going to say," he said when I paused and seemed far away.

"Sorry father, I was thinking, wouldn't it be nice if we were still in the fifties."

"Why do you say that, I think we are better now."

I couldn't evade the question anymore." I was thinking of the Cinema Parrocchiale and how busy we were."

He knew what I meant, instantly he knew I was referring to the time when he was censoring every single film coming in to that cinema and he knew that I knew of all the re-arranging.

"Ho! You still remember", he replied with a smile and a little embarrassment.

"In those days," continued Padre Zoda, "we had two cinemas in Serradifalco as you well know and they were full all the time. They are both gone now. Television has taken over and no one knows what will come on the screen from one minute to the other. He was right there, in that the TV was unpredictable.

Padre Zoda was from Villalba, a town in the vicinity. He came to Serradifalco in the mid-fifties when the former parish priest died. He had a charming way of doing things, a charming way of talking with people and to people. He made a lot of friends very soon, he became very popular in no time but after a few years he also made many enemies. He somehow got involved in politics with the Christian Democratic Party and that was the cause of so many of his friends turning their back on him.

I was a long-time member of the G.I.A.C. (Young Italian Catholic Association), so I was one of the first to welcome him.

In 1952 I was voted president of the Serradifalco G.I.A.C. for the term 1952-56 and then again 1956-60. For both terms Padre Zoda recommended to the bishop that my election be validated. The president of such an association must be elected by the members and recommended to the bishop by the parish priest.

Padre Zoda's good relations with the public didn't last long. By the end of the fifties a sort of resentment had emerged mostly from people with political connections. The peculiar thing was that no one could explain the phenomenon. The phenomenon about the priest was that he was a very clever man, he had entered the political circle without committing himself, playing his part behind the scenes. At first it went unnoticed but then he went more open and it was then that his friends distanced him and a sort of hate started fermenting between the priest and the people.

People would say to me "I hate that man." And when I asked, "Why?" they couldn't answer, they didn't know why. They looked as if they had lost their speech. In the end they would say, "Oh he hasn't done anything to me personally". Others were claiming that he liked money too much, he would do anything for money, or he shouldn't get involved in politics. Really, that was a way out of embarrassment. They were only repeating what they heard from somebody else.

I must say that the priest was politically inclined, but I think he was entitled, as a man, to have his views. He liked money, but, well, who doesn't?

Compare Ingnazio also joined the G.I.A.C. He was the Treasurer, without spending power, at the time when I was President. He too was a great friend of Father Zoda.

"Oh, compare", said Padre Zoda, trying to tease Ingnazio, "what do you think of compare Angelo's surprise visit?"

Ingnazio replied, "Very nice of him, do you think we should organise a party while he is here? It would be a good occasion for old friends to get together."

Compare Ingnazio said this jokingly, knowing the priest didn't like such things.

Father Zoda asked me to go and visit him again before I returned to Canada. He had some photos of New York he wanted to show me. Unfortunately I never found the time to see him again. I thought I would pay him another surprise visit in the future. That was the last I saw of him, poor man. He was so well received when he first came to Serradifalco, nobody would ever think he would have gone that way. I liked him to the end. Although he upset me a few times, I still liked him.

By the end of the seventies Padre Zoda was on his way out.

When the rumour of his activities reached the bishop it was decided that something thing must be done. A newly ordained priest, a native of Serradifalco, was appointed to take his place. The parishioners, of course, were very happy with this decision. Padre Zoda returned to his place of origin where he continued as an archpriest. He must have been in his seventies at that stage. He went to Serradifalco from time to time to visit old friends. I never had another chance to speak to or see him again and find out what really happened.

Soon after my arrival back in Serradifalco I was offered the job I had left but since I hadn't decided whether to stay or leave, I neither accepted nor turned it town. My mother and all the family were saying nothing on the subject. But I am sure they were hoping that I would stay. They were very disappointed when one morning I said, "I'll be going back next week." So after four weeks in Serradifalco, I went back to Montreal. I felt sorry for my mother and for all the family, for that matter, as soon as I left the house, but I had made up my mind and they accepted it.

Once in Montreal, I decided that there must be some changes and adjustment. I approached my employer, pressing him for another increase. He didn't like it. I didn't think he would. In the meantime I was looking for another job. I realised that my expenses were going up noticeably fast. I had stayed in the apartment when my sister went back to Italy and now had to pay the full rent and all the bills to go with it, whereas, when I was with my sister, she only asked for a minimum weekly payment just to cover the cost of my food. I got an increase. It was not satisfactory at all, but it was a start.

Meanwhile I met June. In time we were engaged and eventually we married. We were married at La Chiesa del Carmelo, an Italian Catholic Church in Dante Alighieri Street in Montreal. The church is in a large Italian community which was established at the beginning of the nineteen hundreds. Our wedding reception was held at the Holiday Inn Hotel on Sherbrook Street in downtown Montreal. About one hundred guests attended, including my uncle, aunt and cousin from Schenectady in New York State in the United States and June's parents from England. These were the only relatives able to come for the wedding. It was very good of them to come and I appreciated it very much. We spent two week's holiday touring the New England States, in the US.

On my return to work I found that Mr. Mandel had increased my pay as a wedding present. It was nice of him, I appreciated it and it was a very kind gesture.

One day while I was at work a man came to see me. He introduced himself as Leo and then said, "Mr. English would like to see you."

Charlie English owned the Charles English Ornamental Ironwork Company in another part of the City.

"How did you find me and what does Mr. English know about me?" I asked

"Through Silvio, you know Silvio don't you? He works for Charles English", he replied

That explained it all.

"Why didn't Silvio call me himself?" I said.

"Huh, I can't answer that. Shall I tell Mr. English that you are interested?" he continued.

"That depends on what he offers."

"I'm sure you will like the offer. Shall I say see you at the weekend?
We work until 12 o'clock on Saturday."

The man then left looking very pleased at having convinced me..

The following Saturday I went to see Mr. English. On entering the premises I asked for him.

"Over there" a voice from behind answered, "That's him".

I looked and I saw the man himself coming towards me.

"Hello," he said welcoming me, "You must be Capritta. I'm Charles English. I was expecting you."

We went upstairs into the office, a room high up overlooking the shop floor.

"Sit down please," he said indicating a chair on the other side of the desk.

"Silvio told me about you and what you can do. He also said you are considering leaving Barzel's."

He continued knowingly, "I thought you might be interested in working for me. We've got plenty of work and the firm offers good rates of pay. You can start on Monday if you like."

In Montreal and indeed in all Canada the rates of pay were at the employer's discretion. If the skill of a man or a woman is required then money is the easy part. It seemed to me that Charles English was well informed.

"Thank you, Mr. English, for your generous offer. As you know I have a certain responsibility at Barzel's. Being in charge as you know makes it a bit difficult to leave at such short notice."

He replied, "Oh! I'm well aware of that, if it is a financial matter I'll cover that. I'm sure our rate will cover it."

He knew what the rates at Barzel's were, but he didn't know the rate for being a working foreman.

"May I ask what the average pay is in the shop?" I asked.

"Certainly," he replied. "The average pay in the shop is $3.50 an hour (1966 rates) but for you, I've got something else in mind. Come, I'll show you around the shop and you can meet the men."

We went downstairs where I met some of the workforce including Silvio. The company was desperate for skilled workers. This was the time when the trade fair 'Expo 67' in Montreal was being built and as the date was approaching he was getting more and more nervous.

It was nearly lunchtime and people were getting ready to go home. I took the opportunity to have a word with Silvio.

"Well, thanks again Mr. English, I will let you know one way or the other," I concluded, walking towards the car.

"And of course," Charlie said, "after working hours you can do your own jobs. Goodbye."

"That will suit me very well," I said to myself.

He gave no indication of what I would be doing, or of the specific programme he had in mind but by all accounts he had a plan, perhaps a special team to work at Expo 67.

At the time I was helping to produce some new items for Barzel's to take to a show in three weeks' time. This was a national show held annually in London (Ontario) where all the metal furniture makers took their products. So at least for that period I couldn't leave. It wouldn't have been fair of me if I did that.

I thought it over in the coming weeks. I took everything into consideration, including the money. My pay would go up 50% not including what Mr English had in mind. I decided that I would leave Barzel's.

One morning I went into the office to see Mandel. I told him that I had found another job and I would be leaving shortly. He didn't like it but he understood.

In Canada at the time there was no law of notification to leave. Anyone could come and go at any time. Likewise an employer could at any time go to an employee and tell him or her that his or her work was no longer required.

Later I called Mr English and told him that I would be taking up employment the following Monday, which I did.

At that time construction of Expo 67 was keeping Montreal busy. Charles English had a contract to fabricate and install ironwork at the American and Polish pavilions. The site of Expo 67 was on Saint Helen's Island, an island in the middle of the Saint Lawrence River, just across the many bridges from Montreal.

In 1967 Josephine was born, a big event for us all and what a lovely girl. Quiet and energetic in the daytime but in the night it was a different story. As I was getting ready for bed, Jo was getting ready to wake up. As I got into bed she started screaming at the top of her voice until I went to pick her up. She wouldn't stop unless I kept walking. When the time was approaching for me to go to work Jo went to sleep. That went on for three weeks. After that things were back to normal.

Later in the year Expo 67 opened its doors after years of work which kept Montreal in full employment and abundant wealth. A big event for the City, it was a great success, a show that really put Montreal on the map. Millions of people from all over the world visited it. The pavilions representing many countries were magnificent. After the exhibition most of the pavilions were dismantled, some were left permanently and used for various shows.

That same year, an extremist group emerged, which was not a surprise to anybody. It was a fermenting patriotism, which became open perhaps at the wrong time, it came out prematurely. Some French Canadians thought that things were not moving fast enough towards a free Quebec. The Province of Quebec came under the legislation of the Canadian government.

The idea grew mostly after a brief visit from General de Gaulle, the French President, when in a public speech in front of a large crowd he said, "Vive la belle Province. Vive le Quebec libre." It was a slogan that didn't go down well except with the separatists. It caused a lot of discomfort for the government at the time; it caused offence and embarrassment.

The vast majority of Quebecois wanted to separate from the rest of Canada. They wanted radical reforms including the abolition of the English culture. They wanted French schools, not English ones; they wanted only French-speaking government offices and not English. They wanted only the French language to be spoken in shops, hospitals, banks and all public services.

Bombing went on and disorder of all sorts to destabilise the government and to put pressure on the Parti Quebecois: the political party for Quebec Libre, with Rene Levesque as leader. In 1968 the extremists intensified their campaign with explosions and kidnapping. They abducted Mr. Pierre Laporte the minister of employment for the provincial government, and also James Cross, a British diplomat. Laporte was later killed accidentally while in the hands of the kidnappers. He had been put into the boot of a vehicle and was later found dead. James Cross was freed when the abductors were assured of free conduct to Cuba.

I remember the day when it all happened, in minutes the news spread throughout Canada and across the world. For the separatists, the kidnapping of Laporte and Cross was a fatal mistake, they had taken things too far and for the authorities it was more than they could take. These events were televised from the moment the police circled the area where the separatists' cell was located in the north of Montreal right down to Saint Helen's Island where a helicopter was waiting to take them to Dorval Montreal International airport and then to Cuba.

The City was in a state of alert. An emergency act had to be passed first to protect the citizens and then to eradicate the remaining cells still at large. The National Guard joined the police and they covered the City. While their presence was quite disturbing people felt reassured at the sight of the police and the troops. Despite this action French Canadians proceeded to elect Rene Levesque to power. He became Prime Minister of Quebec unseating Mr. Burassa who was premier before him.

They were calling for one culture and one tongue. They wanted only French-speaking schools to be the sole education in the province. They wanted the abolition of bilingual schools. People were speculating that if, after a Parti Quebecois victory, business people left Quebec they wouldn't be able to take their assets with them. They had thrown the whole system into turmoil.

Banks, insurance companies and others large corporations started moving assets to other provinces such as Ontario, Vancouver, Manitoba and many others and even to the United States of America, before it was too late.

After a while there was a change of heart and things started normalising again but the damage was done. Shareholders were very angry; they were blaming what happened for their loss of millions on the stock markets. Evidently most of the business in Montreal was in the hands of non-French-Canadian people and if they had moved it would have proved disastrous for Quebec. If the new 'would be' constitution were to be implemented it would have been very bad for Quebec and perhaps for the whole of Canada.

1968 was a bad year for Charles English, he went into liquidation despite his efforts to prevent it. One morning before he announced the bankruptcy, he went around the shop making notes of what he had on the premises. That very morning he was wearing his dark glasses. Usually when he had his dark glasses on he had some bad news, in fact anybody could see that something big was coming.

A few months before he had asked everyone to take a fifty cent an hour cut. He explained that if we didn't accept he would have to make some of the men redundant. So we accepted hoping that we would continue working and keep the job secure. But we knew as well as he did that fifty cents wouldn't make much difference to the many thousands of dollars that he owed to suppliers. He was desperate, he didn't know what to do to avoid the embarrassment. He was a serious man and he was ashamed of what had happened. Evidently he was trying to avoid losing the business he had built up in the past twenty years.

A week or two later after adding everything up he thought it was time to make his mind up and come out with it. So he sent his foreman out to ask a few of us to go into the office before we went home to see him one by one. For the rest of the employees, the foreman gave it to them straight, "From Monday" he said, "we are all on holiday." He explained that Mr. English was sorry for all the people concerned but there was nothing he or anyone else could do that he hadn't already done, to prevent what was about to happen.

To those of us in the office Charles English said: "As from Monday we shall be closed. From that date the bailiffs will decide what to do with the premises. If you wish to continue to work for me leave your name and your telephone number before you go." He continued openly: "The outcome from Expo 67 was not as good as it had looked. We should have never taken those jobs on. Anyway we must forget what had happened and look forward." He went on, "We are thinking of opening another place soon, Franz, Giorgio and me, perhaps next week or perhaps next month."

"Here is your cheque, "he said to me, "If I were you I would go to the bank today. I can't guarantee it for next week. Goodbye."

Giorgio was an Italian who had worked for Charles English for some years. Franz was a German and a senior adviser to English and had been with the company longer than Giorgio. Without Franz and Giorgio, Charles English wouldn't have any chance of reopening, he wouldn't know where to start, he was a good businessman but he didn't know a thing about ironwork, in fact he didn't know a thing about manual work. I was astonished to hear all this but not surprised. So before I left I gave my name and my telephone number to the foreman.

It was Friday. Luckily banks usually stay open in Montreal until 8pm on Fridays to give people time to cash their cheques since almost everybody got paid by cheque. So after dinner I went to cash my cheque as suggested. Those who went on Monday were disappointed.

Charles English had taken the Expo 67 work because others did so. As a matter of fact he didn't have the tools for the job. He didn't have the machinery required for the job, heavy and modern machinery such as lifting equipment which he had to hire. He didn't have enough experienced people at the drawing board. Many of the manual workers didn't have a clue about that sort of work therefore mistakes were made, resulting in a waste of time and resources such as money and technical experience which were limited. The timing had been misjudged. As the date for the opening of Expo was approaching he realised that he couldn't deliver. He had to employ more people to implement a night shift.

That alone was a big misjudgement by his aides. At the time it was not easy to find manpower as other companies were rushing to finish on time. He had to pay through the nose if he were to deliver on time and avoid paying some sort of penalty. Almost everybody benefited from Expo 67, but for Charles English it meant disaster. He had lost what he had accumulated in the twenty years he had been in business.

English was a Polish man who had emigrated to Canada soon after the war when Poland became a communist country under the umbrella of the Soviet Union. I never could make him out, in the three years that I worked for him. Nobody I knew saw him either smile or enter into a conversation of any sort other than a business one. He was a very sad man especially on the day he called us into the office to reveal the sad news of the liquidation. Jachek, his right-hand man, was there with him, to support him I assumed. He was his fellow countryman who was as worried as Charlie English was because he was about to lose his job. Jachek had just a few years to go so for him it meant early retirement. He had gone to Canada at the same time as Charlie and when the business started they started work together, Charlie as the owner and Jachek as a superintendent. Neither of them knew a thing about the business they were running.

Charlie and General Jaruzelski, the ex-president of Poland, look alike; they walk the same way, they talk in the same way, they wear the same dark glasses and they would pass for twins. Every time I see the General on television, I see Charlie and relive old memories.

After the bad news I thought I would use the time to have one or two weeks' holiday while I was waiting for Charlie and partners to reopen; or if this didn't happen I would go and look for another job. It didn't work that way. It never does when you want it to. On the following Friday, a week after the old place closed, I received a phone call from Giorgio, one of the three partners. Giorgio was an ambitious young man and getting into that business was just what he wanted; he was the number three man in Charles English's business after Bambace and Franz.

"Hello Angelo," he said, "This is Giorgio. I'm pleased to let you know that we've got a new place. If you are still interested we will be glad to give you your job back."

"Thank you Giorgio," I said, "I'm pleased to hear that. Yes, I am interested."

I could picture him grinning, it was just what he had always wanted to hear and I was pleased that he had got the business started, after all he had the skills and the capacity for the job on the bench, more than Charlie had in the office.

Giorgio was good at job valuations and good in dealing with customers. Franz's task was to get the work done in time and he was very particular about the quality of the work. For him only quality counted. As from the first week, everybody had been asked to take a $10 pay cut and for full co-operation to help the company get on its feet to make sure it succeeded.

Later that year we went to Italy and of course to England because June's family were there, June being English. We met in Montreal by chance. All her family were in England and still are. We usually took four weeks' holiday to have plenty of time with our families. This time we had Jo with us. Although she was very young she was no trouble at all.

In 1969 Margaret was born, another lovely girl. Unlike Josephine, Margaret was quiet night and day - until she started talking and then… It was a pleasure to hear her speak. Jo and Margaret were very nice to one another and still are. They never had a fight and they never disagreed on anything, just the odd scuffle now and then.

In 1970 we went again to Italy and England. This time for my brother's wedding in Caltanissetta. We had Jo and Margaret with us. They enjoyed every minute of it and so did we despite the intense heat. Sicily has a steady temperature of 28 degrees centigrade during July, and until the middle of August with odd days of 35-40C, then as from 15th of August it starts cooling down notably to 18-20C by the end of October when the rainy season is due to start.

It was great to be home once more with family and friends. Sad though to hear sometimes, out of the blue, the names of so many people who had died in the past years I had been away. I found it astonishing to hear the names of people I knew - friends and relatives -many of them young, going the way they did.

One day when I paid my usual visit to the cemetery, I was going through rows of tombs and I found that so many young people I went to school with and whom I knew long after that, had died whether accidentally or from cancer and other diseases. It was distressing to see the names of people I had known and whom I would meet in the public square - they were gone forever. The tombs carried moving words which made you think and realise to what extent life can be stretched. This particular writing on a memorial marble stone read: "Here lies a man who overworked all his life for the well-being of his children, who now pray for his eternal rest."

The man was a relative of ours. He worked non-stop until he died. He had four children and his aim was to give each one a house. He had succeeded in this just before he died. I had last met him a few years before he died. He had had two operations and I asked him how he felt. He answered jokingly, "Oh I haven't got time to think about it, I've got more important things to think about."

"Things like work?" I jokingly asked, meaning the work he had taken on.

"Work" he said, "does not kill people."

"It does not leave them very much alive either," I answered.

We both knew it was a joke so we laughed and changed the subject. We went into a nearby café for an espresso before we parted. He died a year or two later when he had another operation that wasn't successful. He was in his early sixties. He didn't enjoy his life at all nor did his family. In his life there was no room for enjoyment.

I'm very critical of the old traditions in Sicily.

I believe that a man has to do whatever has to be done in order to improve on past generations and to make it possible to hand over to the next generation the best there is, within limits but not over-reaching for the impossible.

In Sicily, like anywhere else, parents do what they can to ensure the future of their children. Parents more than anything else want to see their children get a good start in life. The children in turn do what they can to please their parents for they know family comes first. In Sicily and parts of Southern Italy, when a girl is born parents start thinking about buying her the dowry and so they do, little by little. By the time the girl is old enough to be married the dowry is complete. Of course if the parents are wealthy the dowry can be bought at a later date.

The dowry would consist of a complete range of household items such as several sets of bed linen and towels and all other types of household linen, the idea being that the couple start married life without money worries. The groom's parents usually buy the furniture and the bride's parents aim to provide a house.

Etiquette is still there and very much alive. A man would jump to his feet to make room for a woman or an older person wherever it happened to be. A man would walk down the street on the woman's left side or if he was walking with an older man, he would still walk on the left.

One can almost see whether a couple is married or not. Married couples act differently, there are some disparities between married and unmarried couples. Married couples are very much alike, predictable. In some cases it seems as if they are made for one another. Notably the man is taller and older (six to ten years between them), they act and walk more responsibly and seriously than the others.

Marriage traditions are still in existence though not to the extent that they were.

When a man reaches the age for settling down, between the age of twenty and thirty generally, he starts looking for the girl of his life. These days things have changed, not very much, but things have changed. He more or less knows who his parents would like to see him with, so he does whatever is possible to find someone who will please him and the family. The young women do things in the same way. Unfortunately things can't always be done this way.

When a young couple decide to marry the young man will tell his parents. His mother approaches the girl's mother and asks her, on behalf of his son, for the hand of her daughter. The girl's mother would say that she will have a word with her husband and daughter and will give an answer in due course. Of course, nowadays these things are just formalities, but even so many people would like to keep to the tradition.

Then the obvious and predictable answer comes and a date for an engagement party is set to exchange diamonds and offer the chance for the families of both sides to meet each other. As I pointed out, nowadays these are all formalities. Many decades ago the pattern was the same but the story was different. I won't go into many details, I'll keep it for my next book.

After the usual three weeks in Italy we flew to England. After a two and a half hour flight we landed. We had gone from the heat to the rain and chilly weather, from noisy crowds to the quiet and from pizza to fish and chips. It was 30 degrees centigrade when we left Palermo - it was 12 degrees when we landed at London Heathrow. No matter when we went to England we were greeted with rain and chilly weather throughout the period we were there. It was not until we settled in the country that I realised that it didn't rain all the time and the weather could be very pleasant though rarely hot.

Back to Montreal and back to square one. We realised that buying four tickets to visit our families in Europe was getting a bit too much. We were homesick and that didn't do any good, it didn't help the economic side and financially it was getting a bit uncomfortable. We couldn't stay more than two years away from home. It was like working for the airlines, so we decided that the next trip would be a one way ticket. With that in mind we started working towards the idea of returning.

I liked Montreal, we all liked it, I had a good job and I was good at it. We came to the conclusion that my ambition of working full-time for myself couldn't be realised in the foreseeable future. The girls were growing up fast and if we left it any longer it would become more difficult.

In Canada and indeed in North America it's almost impossible to start any small business and work your way up. Over there everything is big, starting small means staying small. Starting a big business is risky. So I thought of coming to Europe. I thought I would do as well as I did over there.

In 1972 my mother came to Montreal for a four week visit. We showed her around the usual places of interest in Montreal, places like Saint Joseph's Oratory and shrine to Brother Andre, the botanical park and other places of interest.

Montreal has a lot to offer tourists and residents, in winter and in the summer. It has the old and the new, the historical and the contemporary; something for everyone.

On week two of my mother's stay we went to the United States to visit relations in Buffalo, which is not far across the border crossing point at Niagara Falls. Buffalo (New York State) is situated at the eastern end of Lake Erie.

The nearest crossing point into the USA from Montreal is about forty miles which makes it very convenient to go over to visit New England. We often went down to Lake Champlain in Vermont.

After a day or two in Buffalo we continued on to visit my Uncle Gaetano and Auntie Caroline in Schenectady (N.Y. State) where they lived for sixty years before moving to Florida. Schenectady is a lovely town with a long history. We stayed with them for two days. They took us to some places up in the hills to see historic Indian remains and have a picnic in an adjoining park. We also visited a shrine to a young female Indian martyr.

In 1973 we sold up and left Montreal to return to Europe. We landed in England and stayed with June's parents to begin with. I spent time looking to see what the prospects of work and accommodation might be. Prospects seemed good in general but I also wanted to see how things were going in Italy. We went to Italy for several weeks and I explored the possibility of staying there. The prospects were good there also, as in England. Now was the time to decide. Taking everything in consideration we decided to settle in England.

At the time it was not difficult for me to find employment. We stayed with my wife's family in Warwickshire for a short time until we had fully decided to stay.

I started work with GEC Mill Road, Rugby, for just over £19 a week, a drop of 125% compared with the job I had in Montreal. I felt like packing again, but I had to give myself more time. So I did and after a long wait I established myself a reasonable week's pay.

We went through the summer and through the winter. The weather was better than I expected. 1974-75 followed with soaring temperatures, plenty of sunshine in the summer months and mild in the winter. It was just as I wanted it to be. Then came the winter again, with rain, wind and snow. The winter went and the spring came, it brought hard frost and freezing wind. The following summer was a 'typical English summer' people said, with quite a lot of rain.

Once established in work we settled in Monks Kirby, a village near Rugby. The girls were enrolled at Saint Joseph's RC First School in the village. My wife took a part time job in the same school, which was very lucky and convenient for us all.

We were getting used to the idea that the time for running about was over. We continued to go to Italy every summer for our four week's holiday in July-August. This went on until 1980 when I started working for myself. Then everything changed. We had to adjust ourselves again to a new way of life, to a new way of doing things, and to arrange our future plans - from the daily routine to the annual holiday.

In 1978 came bad news at GEC Mill Road. The first group was made redundant. In 1979 we were told in the tinsmiths shop that closure was imminent. The management, through a representative of our union, explained that work was scarce, insufficient to keep the workforce of about twenty in the tinsmiths. The real scarcity of work was created by the management; they were sending work out to be done more cheaply. By doing that they were starving the tinsmiths which would force the closure.

Was there a real urgency for closing the tinsmiths? Yes there was. A few years earlier the management had introduced a new scheme, which in my opinion was inappropriate. The scheme gave us a substantial increase. It was good for us, in the tinsmiths, our earnings went up considerably but that was bad news for the company. They thought and realised that we were getting too much money for the work we were doing and since there was no going back, the only way to terminate the scheme was the closure of the tinsmiths.

In May of the same year redundancy notes were served to all but three of us in the tinsmiths. The notes read: with much regret we the management at GEC give notice that after the July-August shutdown the tinsmiths will remain closed indefinitely.

We already knew from a previous meeting all the details about redundancy, etc. Wondering about my note, I went to see Mr. Burton the then superintendent for the tinsmiths and fabrication. I wanted to know why my note was not with the others.

Mr. Burton said, "You, Peter and Eric will be transferred to fabrication." I was not pleased at all with the news. I didn't like the place and I didn't like the work in that building. I told him that I didn't like the plan, I wasn't part of it, and that I didn't think I would like the work.

He replied, "You have nothing to worry about. You, Peter and Eric will be doing the same job you have been doing in the past seven years with the same money, the same conditions, but in a different building, and I guarantee that."

"Why don't you let me out of your plan?" I asked once more.

"I can't," he answered. "If I let you go I'll have to look for somebody else to replace you."

I was far from convinced, I didn't believe in his guarantees, for I knew once in fabrication things would change, and anyway if I had wanted to work in fabrication, I would have done so from the start.

The General Electric Company entered the eighties going downhill and I was worried. I was worried because time was going by fast and I thought the time was right to do what I had wanted to do for a very long time. That was my main reason for wanting to leave the works. The way things were going even the job in fabrication was not secure. Considering my age it was better if I went, so I could more easily start again while I was young enough, whereas three, four or five years later it would be more difficult for me to initiate any business of my own.

Looking back, in Serradifalco things were going badly as well. Redundancies and the closure of establishments were on the way too. I called it an international epidemic.

"Restructuring of industry" people at the higher level called it, they were manipulating a solid structure, shaking the well-established roots of what was vital for all, at the expense of the people in general.

The management accused the unions of not co-operating to fight competition, accused them for not doing more to compete with giant industries whose production was no match for smaller establishments. The unions in turn were saying that the fault lay at management level. They took advantage of the policies of the time and the money made available by the Common Market or something similar topped up by the government.

The friends I spoke to were in a state of confusion. They were talking according to which union they were in. Really I could understand people backing the scheme, there was a lot of money involved and many were looking forward to it. Many put up a fight but they knew that they were fighting a losing battle. For they knew that the future of their children was at an end and that the economy which was going so well risked being reversed.

The job in fabrication was getting more and more as I'd predicted, work was diminishing day by day. In my first six months there I never did a job similar to the one in the tinsmiths. They started to push Eric, Peter and me from one end of the place to the other. We were doing odd heavy dusty jobs, evidently none of the tinsmith jobs were coming in. Peter and Eric were putting up with it, for they had not many years to go before retirement. I was not prepared to do so, I had to find a way to get out and fast. I knew that it was nobody's fault that things were going bad at Mill Road but I just wanted to go, have a fresh start.

I decided to go and see Mr. Burton again who had promised me my type of work. As usual there had been a change of guard. He was no longer at the office; he had been transferred to another department. I guessed that Mr. Burton's transfer was part of the scheme. I understood how he would have felt to face people whom he had promised things that he could not deliver.

I spoke with Mr. Burton's replacement. I told him the story, but he already knew. He told me what the position was and I asked him if it would be possible for him to include my name in the next redundancy list.

He said, "I'm not in a position to do so, but I'll see what I can do."

"If you really want to leave the job why don't you resign," he suggested.

"I don't think I'll do that, goodbye," I said and I left feeling very annoyed.

Resigning would have been the easy way out, but if I did I would not be entitled to redundancy money so I decided to wait.

In the spring of 1980, GEC announced a number of redundancies in the fabrication shop and in some of other departments. This time my name was included. In a way I was pleased, pleased to leave the most unpleasant place I had ever worked in, as the practical conditions were concerned. On the other hand I liked working for the firm.

So in May that year I left GEC and was ready to start on my own. In September of the same year I started my business, Newton Forge in Newton near Rugby. I took over the old forge which had been closed for many years.

A few days after opening, I had people come from the "Rugby Advertiser" and from "Radio Mercia" as soon as they knew that a business was taking off. Evidently, the then local Member of Parliament, when he found out about Newton Forge opening, had informed the press. Presumably at the time he was taking some pride in a new business starting, especially in and around his constituency.

The "Advertiser" wrote a very good article on the Forge's past history and its revival. "Radio Mercia" announced that Newton Forge has been revived after 25 years of closure. The forge first opened in the middle of the nineteenth century and when the last owner died in 1955 it remained closed until 1980 when I came to the rescue!

The publicity given by the "Advertiser" and "Radio Mercia" brought customers to the Forge and I was off to a good start with orders for the wrought ironwork I was producing.

The business continued well and many satisfied customers came back with more orders. It gave me great pleasure when customers came and told me that they couldn't find anybody to do the job. Perhaps this was because I was able to make one-off pieces to specification.

It was good to know that I was my own boss and that I didn't have to answer to anybody, except the taxman!
Because of my new enterprise, we had to rearrange our annual

holiday. No more four weeks' holiday in August but one week now and then.

In the mid-eighties during one of our trips to Italy, I found that most of my friends were retired millionaires, in lire that is to say! A year or so earlier the government had passed a bill that gave employees the right to retire if they had fifteen years' service and were forty-five years of age. They could go with 80% pay and a good deal of redundancy money. This law applied only to people working in the mines of Serradifalco and the surrounding area. To me this was a law tailored to shut down the works with an offer no one could refuse. So they took the offer.

Redundancy averaged from 50 to 100 million Italian lire (25-50 thousand pounds sterling) 80% of the previous year's earnings plus an accumulative bonus - that is one week's pay for every year a man or a woman worked for a firm. This sort of agreement was to continue until a better solution was found.

The agreement mentioned above meant that if a person had worked for 20 years when he retired he would get 20 weeks extra pay from his or her employer. The rate of payment would reflect his changing salary over 20 years' service.

The scheme had been put in place by the government a few years earlier to encourage employees to stay with the same firm for longer. If they changed job they would lose the bonus weeks they had accumulated.

The deal offered by Montecatini was a very good one for those who accepted, but a bad one for future generations. As of today (1990) 25% of the workforce, or perhaps less, is left still working just to keep the place going, to prevent the water rising in case the firm had a second thoughts, changed its mind and opened the works again. They are all young men working there who do not yet qualify for the deal.

It won't be long before the place which was built 35 years ago with so much enthusiasm and so much hope will close indefinitely. The economy in the region is expected to maintain its pace until the 'millionaires' are gone, for they will cease to draw the great pensions which, for the moment, benefit the youngsters too.

This was the result of a wasteful society, the result of the industrialists' selfishness, with a helping hand from people at a higher level. They dig into the ground, take the easy portion and leave the rest in the ground where it will be lost forever. They jump from one place to another to take what is easy for the sake of growing popular, rich and prestigious. They leave behind ruins, bitterness and discontentment.

A few died in the making of the place and a lot more were injured for life. All of those who had good and bad experiences will tell the story in their own way. There will be only one end to the story, the place will close when it shouldn't have and never open again. Those who died believed that sacrificing their lives was for the benefit of the growing workforce of the community.

The ones who were injured had a sense of pride, something that they couldn't explain themselves, yet were proud of having built something that 30 years earlier would have been unthinkable.

A team of enthusiasts who had the history of the works at heart got together and salvaged what they could. They gathered as much information as there was available and put it in the library building where future generations will learn about Serradifalco's cultural and material past. They will learn about their ancestors and what they did for a living. They will learn what life was like in the history of mining which spans a few centuries.

This, our recent trip to Sicily, was somehow different, different because we didn't have the children with us. Different because we managed to visit where we couldn't get to before and different because we did what we wanted to do as we thought of it. We found my mother reasonably well; she has a lot of energy, considering that at times she is very ill.

My brother Pino's wife Elisa recovered well after a stroke she had in March 1990, a very serious one; it had put her life in a very serious condition, it required immediate open-heart surgery. She still needs medical attention and a lot of family care.

Pino and his wife have five children - four girls and one boy, five lovely children, Giusi, Sara, Claudia, Maria Pia and Paolo. One of the girls, Giusi, the oldest, was married to Salvatore in September this year (1990).

The wedding was on 18th September, a wedding we didn't want to miss, but unfortunately for various reasons we were not able to be there. Our youngest daughter attended the wedding and afterwards travelled north to Urbino where she was on a year's student exchange at the University of Urbino studying Italian.

Prior to the wedding, by coincidence at the same time as our holidays, Pino rented a villa at the seaside for all his family. This was next door to my brother Enzo's villa in Falcone in the province of Messina. So we joined them, my mother, my wife and me. We had a lovely week, a week I will never forget. I couldn't remember the last time so many of us were able to be together. There were fifteen of us; eight were youngsters (my nieces and nephews) aged from fourteen to twenty-five.

Enzo and his wife Franca loved their seaside place, a villa twenty km from Milazzo where they lived permanently and where their two children Paolo and Salvatore attended school. Paolo and Salvatore are as lovely as Pino's children, they love the family. They use the villa two months in the year-July and August- and the odd weekend in the course of the year.

Like many good things our week came to an end rather quickly. It was time to go back to Serradifalco, about three hours away by train.

In Serradifalco, nobody talks anymore about the closure of the works; perhaps they feel somehow ashamed after losing what was for the town a future asset. Consequently, not only the men and women who worked there had to give up their jobs, but the growing generation also had to forget about their future dream, their hope of taking employment with the mighty Montecatini, one of the biggest employers in Italy.

But in this good old town some things never change, things like traditional religious feasts which are there as they always have been, unspoiled by the modern revolution. People look forward to these traditional feasts and when the bell tolls everybody is ready to join in and enjoy every minute of it.

Cafes are very popular now, they are as popular as the wine shops were in the old days. Wine shops these days are almost extinct, people nowadays drink their wine at home. Wine shops and piazze (public squares) used to be social places, now it's cafes and pizzerie.

I met Constantino, a friend of mine, on my way home one evening, after I had left some friends in the piazza. He was a good friend and he took me back some forty years. Constantino was part of a small orchestra we had formed, a casual group I would say, a DIY sort of thing, it consisted of five instruments: an accordion, a clarinet, a guitar, a violin, drums and many singers.

Constantino was himself an instrument, a very peculiar instrument, he used to play with his nose, he used to be very good at it, it is incredible but it is true, he used to make a tune, a very nice tune I must say.

"Hello stranger," he said.

"Hello Constantino, and how are you?" I asked.

"I'm all right old friend and how are you?" he asked coming towards me to shake hands.

"Is your nose still active? Would you be ready for a serenade any time without notes?" I joked.

"Oh yes very much active" he answered (playing a note or two), and at any time.

"We are no longer at that stage, are we Constantino."

"I'm afraid not," he continued, "I remember when all was straight forward, all seemed flat. Now, it is all uphill."

Constantino is getting on now; he must be in his sixties, quite a bit older than I am. He chose to stay single, as head of the family after his father died. He was the only breadwinner so he had to continue to provide for the family (three sisters all single and his old mother). This was one of the reasons he never married.

Constantino was one of the old shoemakers, still working with his bare hands just like they did long ago. He inherited his trade from his father, but unfortunately like many other trades it has almost vanished and now he's doing less and less.

He said when I asked about his shoe business: "These days everybody buys shoes off the shelf. They buy shoes that wear evenly so that, when they are worn it's not worth repairing, so people throw them away and buy a new pair. I can't really blame them, sometimes the repair costs as much as a new pair. Money these days is no longer a problem. Nevertheless there are a few of the old customers who from time to time bring the odd pair of shoes to be mended or buy a pair of new ones. They do me a good turn but I must say they still think of the good old days. They would say, "You can't beat a pair of good handmade shoes."

I would be happy to carry on the trade for many years to come as my father and his father before him. Unfortunately, due to the scarcity of customers causing shortage of work in my trade I have had to look at something else."

"How come you didn't go for expansion, I mean like many others, shoemakers who opened shoe shops and sell new shoes and many other things to go with them?"

"I considered that," Constantino continued, "I considered it some years ago but it came to nothing, I came to the conclusion that there are too many shops in town for so few people.

When we were poor we were content, we were not spoiled. All those years ago we were contented with a little, now we have a lot and still we are not satisfied. There are things people have never seen before, including different types of shoes, things that we don't recognise or know where they come from or what to do with them and yet we buy them. These days we buy everything just because it is there and because we can and money is available.

Now, as I said before, money is not a problem any longer, everybody has a means of transport. They go to the city where they probably pay more for the same merchandise they could get here in town but they are happy to find what they wanted and they enjoy the day out."

"What about all those shoe shops in Serradifalco, they are traditional giabbattini, (shoemakers) it seems to me as if they are doing okay."

"Yes, you are right, they are doing okay, but doing okay is not sufficient, in that sort of business there is a considerable amount of money involved and I was not prepared to risk it. If things go wrong you end up with nothing, I personally didn't have that sort of money and I was not prepared to go to the bank for it. There are some people doing well and there are some people doing not so well. If people are not doing well they are not happy, so they might as well give it up, in fact many have done so."

Compare Carmelo and his brother joined in to say hello, I was shocked at compare Carmelo's appearance, he looked like an old man. I found out later that he was seriously ill with a certain disease which meant that in order to survive he had to have his blood changed every other day, going to hospital regularly for a transfusion. He has been retired now for some time as a result of the disease. Although he knew what his destiny was, he never lost his sense of humour, he started talking about the old days and all that we used to do, about all the friends who were still in Serradifalco and the ones who had left. He was one of the group we had formed, he used to play the clarinet and he was very proud of it.

Compare Carmelo and I have always been good friends, we lived within one or two hundred metres of each other until we were in our twenties, when we both emigrated.

I offered my condolences to Calogero, Carmelo's brother, who had lost his wife a year earlier. Calogero was a teacher at an agricultural college some miles away from home and of course this made it more difficult for him to look after the children, nevertheless it seems that he coped patiently and efficiently. He has two young children, two lovely boys, both at elementary school.

Carmelo and Calogero were in their fifties. Carmelo never married for various reasons concerning the family. It is very sad to see friends or hear about their misfortune, particularly friends you grew up with, especially when suddenly you have to face the reality and talk to them and try to overcome the shock.

I planned to see most of my relatives and friends in my last week on holiday.Unfortunately in the early hours of that last Monday morning a sudden stomach pain awoke me.I was worried, I was very worried for I knew what the matter was, it was my gallbladder, which had tormented me for the past thirty years. I didn't know what to do, I didn't want my mother to know, I didn't want her to worry, so I tried to withstand it while I could. The more time went by the more severe the pain got.

By mid-morning I had to call the doctor, which was no help at all. He gave me some remedies but none of them worked. By Monday afternoon I couldn't wait any longer so I went to the hospital where they kept me for a whole week. The pain itself lasted twenty-four hours but they kept doing tests throughout the week, giving me injections and drips for most of that period. The result: a gallbladder infection. I suppose that was caused by the extra rich food, the extra wine and the extra heat.

I didn't see all the people I wanted to see but I saw many relatives and friends I hadn't seen for many years, they came to see me at the hospital when they heard that I was taken ill. I was not surprised to see them because that is how they are over there. Sometimes you see more people when you are ill than when you are well and looking for them and I was pleased to see them all.

I left the hospital on the Sunday, a day after we were due to leave for England so I contacted the insurance people whom I had kept informed throughout my stay in hospital and they promptly arranged our return flight for the Wednesday. It was all very quick, we didn't have time for anything else but packing. I had hoped for another week's stay. Since at that time of the year the airlines are busy I was keeping my fingers crossed and hoping there were no seats so we could stay a bit longer.

But on the Monday night I received a call from the insurers telling me to be at the airport in Catania for Wednesday morning. He gave me all the instructions and the timetable and that was it. There was no time to say goodbye to my brothers and their families and no time to thank those people who came rushing to see me at the hospital.

My mother was upset because she had something planned. It was very disappointing. Regrettably we had to leave and so we did. It seemed as if there was no time for anything.

The morning before we left I met cousin Leonardo for the first time in thirty years. He was in Sicily to visit his relations. He lives in Mantova now, in the north of Italy, where apparently he found the job he always wanted.

Leonardo started work at a very young age in his father's cava where the work was hard and the money very little. A cava is a pit, an open mine. They were extracting gypsum, a white softy rock that after being broken into manageable pieces was put into a large furnace skilfully placed ready for a long burning session.

Although it was a soft rock it was blasted with dynamite. Then the furnace was lit and fired for eight hours. After eight more hours cooling time it was ground to a fine powder, mixed with a specific amount of ash and was then ready to use. It was widely used for building houses and all sorts of jobs; these days is it called polyfilla. When the builder used it, he mixed it in small quantities at a time because it went as hard as its original state after ten minutes. Gypsum or chalk has become a material of the past. Cement and concrete have taken its place. The "caves" have all gone into liquidation.

Leonardo's father and my father were brothers, and Leonardo and I, apart from being cousins, were good friends. We met every evening in the piazza (public square) where we walked and chatted about the past, the present and the future, making plans of all sorts. He was always talking and moaning about the cava and its hard work. He was not at all pleased with it. In fact when he reached the lawful working age (16 years old) he went to work on a building site and became a builder like the rest of the generation before him. He didn't like this either, and at the first chance he left it.

Our grandfather started this particular cava at the beginning of the century after he settled in Serradifalco. Originally he came from Licata, a town on the southeast coast of Sicily. He came to Serradifalco at the same time as Verderame, the man who took over the sulphur mines about 2 km from the town. Grandfather supplied gypsum to Verderame for use inside and outside the mine. He also provided manpower for the maintenance of the mine; he made sure that maintenance was up to standard, the standard of the time.

In grandfather's era business was quite good, he did well in his life. With the help of his sons he accumulated a small fortune for his seven children. At the time families all pulled together for they knew that was what made the family strong, but in Leonardo's time things were reversed, cement and concrete had taken over from gypsum, an industry that employed hundreds or perhaps thousands of people.

That same morning I also met Michele Territo and then 'compare' Salvatore Augello, long-time friends since school days. Then I met Michele, a teacher and a dedicated politician, who joined the Christian Democratic Party. He became mayor of Serradifalco and was elected for three terms. He was very successful in his career as a politician and as a teacher. I also met Salvatore, who graduated in the mining industry and was also a politician, and who joined the communist party.

The mayor in Italy is voted to power by the people for a four year term, the procedure is the same as in the central government but of course on a much smaller scale. The mayor has to be a good and well-known politician in order to gain the credibility of the people to run, together with the consiglieri (councillors), also elected from the people, the economy and indeed all the affairs of the town or city.

Salvatore is at the town hall seated with the opposition. He has been elected as many times as Michele has. Michele and Salvatore, being poles apart, are in continuous conflict when they are in the chamber facing one another.

I remained neutral although I retain my views, so when we meet we talk about progress, regress, families, work and friends regardless of politics.

At present Michele, as well as being mayor, teaches at the elementary school in Serradifalco.

Salvatore retired from the mine when the works were terminated. He is still leader of the left and a strong activist in the communist party (democratic party of the left it is called now, since last autumn). He has earned the post of general secretary of the USEF which looks after the rights of workers at home and at times of compatriots abroad.

Between the two, in my opinion, there has always been a sense of optimism and fairness.

In Michele, an evident optimism, he is a big man physically with a big heart, modestly generous and friend of all. Salvatore is an equally generous and fair man who always defends the rights of others in a just and legitimate manner. I admire them both for they were doing a good job.

Back in Monks Kirby and back to the usual routine, settling down once again to work. We found Margaret packing up getting ready to leave for Italy where she was to attend the full year at the University of Urbino. She left on 12th September for Serradifalco to stay for two weeks with my mother and to attend her cousin's wedding before proceeding to Urbino. After four weeks in

Urbino she seemed to have settled very well, she likes the people, the town, the weather and the accommodation.

I hope that my mother will live for many years to come for I can go at the present rate to visit her and my friends and my town. Only my mother is left in Serradifalco now. My two brothers have settled in other parts of Sicily.

14120536R00115

Printed in Great Britain
by Amazon